Being "The Other Woman"

by

Petra Falk

The complete handbook for the
woman in love with a married man

This book is dedicated to:

....Carl Heaven, who died April 2007.

You were "The One"

*

....my wonderful ex-husband - so sorry I could
not be the perfect wife for you

*

.... Michele – Poiche tu sei chi sei tu.

*

Je Ne Regrette Rien

Much
can be inferred about a man
from his mistress: In her one beholds
his weaknesses and his dreams.

Georg C. Lichtenberg (1742 – 1799)

Acknowledgments

*T*hank You to all the people who have helped me make this book happen!

My dear, patient and almost always supportive friends, who have stood by me through both the writing of this book and also throughout the times when I needed them to tell me that everything would be ok (whether any of us actually believed it or not), to listen to me (whether they particularly agreed with what they were hearing or not) and to just be there for me, almost without fail and, no doubt, at times with gritted teeth.

Friends like that are vital for everyone, but especially so for a woman writing a book, or having an affair. And most definitely so for a woman insane enough to end up being engaged in both these pursuits at the same time!

I would particularly like to single the very people without whom this whole project would have been doomed from the start... first and foremost the unnamed husbands, wives and mistresses who were generous enough to tell me about their or their husbands' affairs so honestly and candidly. It can't always have been easy for them to admit to certain aspects, or to relive painful periods in their lives. Their contribution to this book was immeasurable and I appreciate their help more than I can say.

Also a great "Thanks" to my friend Jochen, who was so often used as a sounding board on "the male perspective," and who is always there for me (sooner or later, punctuality not being his most outstanding virtue) even though the whole subject of this book does not sit comfortably with his attitude and moral standards at all.

Frankly often the friends who disagree with what you are doing and still firmly stand by you are the most wonderful friends. So, Thank You Jochen, for your friendship and for being critical yet supportive!

Two wonderful generous ladies agreed to do the final editing and did a wonderful job, gently breaking the news to me that "No" – the book was not quite "ready to go" and that I had to grit my teeth and do some more work. Thank You Kristina Lorusso and Rebecca Carlson, without your work and encouragement I really might have chucked it all in just before reaching the finishing line. You're both awesome. Kristina deserves most of the credit for the historical section which was a right mess before she sorted it out.

And – to finish the acknowledgments – Michele, you didn't even know I was writing this book, or rather, you knew I was writing one but not what it was about. You may never know how much your presence in my life has influenced it. *Poiche tu sei chi sei tu* – "Because you are who you are" – indeed!!!!!

Prologue

Almost half of all married men, and slightly fewer married women, admit to having had at least one affair. Amongst those in long term relationships the percentage of those who admit to having strayed at least once is even higher. As this tends not to be something that is too cheerfully admitted to I suspect the real figure may scare the most hardened realist.

I have often heard an "Other Woman" say "But I don't know anyone else who has done this, no-one in my family has, and none of my friends have either." Well, they are very much mistaken. Chances are they know plenty of people who have had, and quite a few who are having, an affair. It's just not something people tell everyone around them.

If the statistics are even remotely accurate we can look at any group of people, anywhere (with the possible exception of a monastery), and roughly half of them will have had an affair at some stage in the lives.

Scary, isn't it? And, at the same time, somewhat reassuring, because however alone we may feel at times with our situation, we are, in fact, not alone at all. We are many. Many more than society as a whole wishes to accept.

There are books about "how to be" just about everything under the sun, but for the woman who more or less unexpectedly finds herself in the situation where she has assumed a role that is rarely spoken about in polite company, there is little help except "Don't do it."

Now this is not particularly helpful when one is in emotional turmoil because things have gone past the point where "Don't go there, it will end in tears, most likely yours" is of any help at all.

This book is not intended to entice nice girls to don a short skirt, slap on the mascara and go on the hunt for a defenseless married man to drag kicking and screaming back to her lair.

It is absolutely not intended to be a "how to become a mistress" book either. Instead it is meant to be a book that will help those who are already finding themselves in this situation to survive doing the least harm to everyone involved, including themselves.

Those who may expect a step-by-step guide on "how to make one's lover leave his wife" will be disappointed I'm afraid. If we have chosen the man wisely, and have conducted our affair with care, love, dignity and intelligence, the above may be the outcome.

I won't promise that it will be in your case. It may be, but the statistics say that the odds are stacked against you.

What I *can* promise you is the following:

If you have chosen wisely, and are taking at least some aspects of this book to heart, you will be better equipped to avoid "blowing it."

Chapters

- 1 -

How a "nice girl" turned into a mistress; My own story

O nce upon a time I was a perfectly normal, happy girl in my thirties, with a great job, a nice home (complete with a lovely husband) in the suburbs, a great social life, dogs and horses, and very little that I could possibly complain about. I was not unhappy in any way, shape or form, there was nothing missing from my life as far as I was aware.

And, as far as the subject matter of affairs was concerned, well, I didn't just sit on the moral high horse, I owned it. Hell, I owned a whole herd of moral high horses. Have an affair? ME? Go anywhere near a married man? No chance! As far as I was concerned, in my probably somewhat complacent state of suburban bliss, having an affair was something nasty devious women did, or unattractive ones who could not get a man of their own. Not the likes of me and my girlfriends, not happy, attractive, smart young women with a great life.

That conviction was dealt its first, but not yet quite fatal blow when my best friend started an affair with a married man. My very beautiful, actually very moral best friend did something I never thought would enter her head.

She, who should have known better, having been at the receiving end of own husband's infidelity, and who had always been so scathing about the type of woman who would as much as entertain the notion of having a fling with a married man.

Her affair ended fairly spectacularly (if I recall correctly much of the final act was played out quite publicly in a plowed field involving very noisy arguments that kept the local gossips in material to sneer about for weeks to come) and was rarely mentioned again, so in my naïve mind all appeared well again in Suburbia.

We were all leading the kind of lives where looking at things like that too closely might just have uncovered the cracks in our pseudo-happy little world, so we just carried on like we had before. Frankly, we were all too busy anyway juggling careers, homes, hobbies and social lives to dwell on "minor indiscretions."

Then I met Carl, who worked in the same building, just a floor below. We'd meet in the smoker's corner first by accident, then probably by design, and started talking. The frequency of my cigarette breaks increased and soon just "happened" to coincide with his by a mixture of subconscious clock-watching and semi-conscious synchronization of our nicotine addiction.

We became friends, and for the best part of 6 months we'd go for a drink, a walk or shopping at lunchtime; talking, laughing, "just friends" for all intents and purposes. Or so we kidded ourselves anyway.

Our colleagues in both companies just "*knew*" we were having an affair many months before we actually did.

The evening when I crossed the line from "friend" to "mistress" will be etched in my mind forever, along with the emotional turmoil it threw both of us into.

The day had started innocently enough. It was just before Christmas and we had somewhat reluctantly agreed to cancel our lunchtime trip to the pub in order to catch up with some Christmas shopping instead, but one of us, and I can not for the life of me remember which one it was, suggested a drink after work instead.

It was the first time we were to meet in the evening, and the first time we did not have the usual restriction of having to be back in the office within an hour, give or take a few minutes. When I drove into Newbury to meet him I clearly remember a faint sense of anticipation as I parked the car, checked my reflection in the rear view mirror one last time and slowly made my way into the pub.

Things were different right from the beginning, as if we both knew that things would probably never be quite the same between us after that evening, whichever way it might end.

I had categorically not planned to start an affair with Carl that day (and I know this to be true because, to be blunt, I would have taken much more care with my choice of undergarments had I as much as entertained the possibility when I got dressed in the morning).

We had a glass of wine or two, we chatted, we looked into each others' eyes just that little bit longer than strictly necessary, and then there was the one moment when the line was crossed and there was no turning back: We had been chatting away in our usual animated manner, and a strand of hair had fallen across my cheek. Carl quite subconsciously (or so he claimed when we dissected that moment at a much later stage) reached across and stroked it gently out of my face.

At just about any time up to that moment I may have had the will to turn back, stop what was happening, return our friendship to what it had started as, and avoided having an affair with a married man.

After that moment there was no way I was going to put a stop to it all. I can not say that I could not have stopped it had I really *wanted* to – but there was no way I could make myself *want to* stop it so I didn't and by the time I got home many hours later I had become a married man's mistress, had cheated on my husband, and to my considerable surprise I did not even feel guilty about it.

That bit actually came as a bit of a shock to me. I had always thought that I would have to be eaten up by guilt, or remorse, or at the very least experience some stirring of a queasy feeling somewhere deep inside where I suspected my conscience to reside.

But all I felt was elation and excitement. I guess the only thing I felt guilty about was the fact that I was not actually really feeling guilty at all. In some of my more self-critical moments I wondered if there was something badly wrong with me because I did not feel guilty, but these thoughts were fairly easily buried under the mass of other emotions and when they did raise their heads I closed the lid on them pretty swiftly until, a few weeks later, gave up their fight and vanished altogether.

The next few months were a rollercoaster like nothing I have ever experienced. I carried on my busy and full life like before, plus a pretty intensive affair, the practicalities and logistics of which showed I possessed both more organizational talent and a considerably greater capacity for deceit than I had ever thought possible.

They also showed that one can drive from the sleepy edges of one county to the great City of Bath in the next county in under an hour given an absence of visible police-cars on the motorway combined with a will to get there before midnight.

I also learned how little sleep a woman needs if her adrenaline level, supported by copious amounts of caffeine, is kept high enough.

I would not want to miss the time that followed for anything. Carl and I had the most perfect "Non-Relationship" imaginable. He was, in my heart at least, my soul mate, my best friend, my lover and the center of my universe.

It all ended in tears of course, mine and his, and those of his wife. Their marriage may have been dead in the water for a while, as his friends confirmed to me years later, but I can't dodge the responsibility of having been a major part of something that caused her great pain, and that (and that part alone) I am sorry for.

The storm crept up on us just as we were beginning to relax a little and became somewhat complacent (there's a lesson in this – do not allow yourself, or your man, to become complacent as that's the first step to being found out.)

In the end it was an innocent snapshot of me playing with my brother's dog that started an avalanche of events that would change the course of not just one, but four lives forever. I had spent some time with my family in Germany and, as one does, brought back photos. One particular picture was Carl's favorite and he asked if he could have it. That in itself was not quite so bad (he lived away from home during the week and all he had to do was not take it with him to the happy home at the weekends), but he was stupid enough to show it to his best friend, who told his own wife, who told her friend, who just happened to be friends with Carl's wife and BOOM – shit hit fan big time.

All hell broke loose in Carl's life and we decided to stop seeing each other for the time being to work out what should happen next. The moment when I heard that "D-Day" (Discovery Day) had descended upon us, and that we should cut all contact for the time being, felled me like a tree. I was in the office, and was actually first shell-shocked, then physically sick. I spent the next few days mustering a steely strength I never thought I had in me just to carry on functioning.

Surprisingly I managed. No one at work or home noticed the state I was actually in.

This break lasted a few weeks and was probably the most emotionally turbulent time I can imagine I will ever have to endure. During this time Carl and his wife tried to make a go of things but really they both knew that their relationship was kaput even before I happened (I would probably not have happened in the first place otherwise anyway).

So they split up, and we were suddenly in a situation where we COULD have been together had we wanted to, but this wasn't the way it was supposed to come about. We both decided that we needed to tidy up our own lives first, he went traveling around the world and I ended my own marriage in an orderly and amicable fashion before going my own way for a while.

I can't help but wonder if that was not a horrible mistake, but at the time we both saw that the situation as it had developed was not a healthy basis for a new, lasting relationship, however strongly we felt about each other.

We wanted to see if we could make a go of things as two free people who could make that commitment, not out of a crazy situation where basically all our hands had been forced.

I was torn at the time but had to admit that I would never really get full peace of mind with the niggling question of whether I had eventually "got him" simply because his marriage had imploded, rather than because of his conscious choice to be with me.

Sadly Carl died in a tragic accident before we got the chance to see if we could have made the transition from having an affair to being a couple.

Whilst I had never wanted to be anyone's mistress, and whilst the concept is still not one I am truly comfortable with, that relationship is one that I will always think back upon with deep affection, with love, and with what a romantic would call "sweet sorrow." I have my memories of an incredible time with a truly wonderful man and I believe I learned a lot from my mistakes.

Would I do things differently if I could turn back the time? The honest answer is that I probably would have changed details, and I would have tried to make sure that we weren't found out. God knows how things would have turned out then.

But even with the 20/20 clarity of hindsight I would almost certainly still have ended up becoming Carl's Other Woman because at the time whatever happened to and between us was just too strong.

Will I ever be someone's mistress again? Well, a few months ago I would have answered with a loud resounding "NO" - like most women with a normal, healthy attitude to relationships, marriage and life in general. Especially one who has "been there, done it, worn the T-Shirt."

However, sometimes things happen when we least expect them to, and whilst it is not a role I have ever craved or even really accepted as something I would deliberately seek out for myself, the fact is that whilst I am sitting here finishing this book there is another tall, dark, handsome and unfortunately very married man in my life yet again.

It wasn't planned like this, I did not mean this to happen, and it is having a profound effect on this book because it was almost finished when I met "M."

Meeting him stopped me in my tracks and I did not as much as look at the book for months. When I dug it out again several months into the course of this affair (what a nasty word for something that feels so "right" ...) I had an overwhelming urge to re-write a lot of the chapters, add a bit here, delete some parts there, and basically include what I had learned in this new situation.

One thing I am quite sure of is that I will never "go there" again − regardless of how this current "relationship" (if you allow me to call it that) pans out in the medium- and long-term. Famous last words? Maybe, but even I will eventually learn from what I can barely bring myself to call "My Mistakes."

Even I will eventually crave (and hopefully get) a relationship that isn't hidden away, and get to be with someone I can call when I feel like just hearing his voice, and hug when I feel like I need a hug, not when it's my turn to be fitted into his schedule.

Hope springs eternal so I can't quite prevent myself thinking that this may just be "*it*" Time will tell and I guess people buy lottery tickets on a daily basis at much smaller odds of hitting the jackpot, so we will just have to wait and see.

In some respects having an affair (and any relationship to a greater or lesser extent) is a bit like childbirth (although I have to confess that I haven't tried the "childbirth" part) in that you remember the good bits and forget about the pain, or rather: You remember that it can hurt but not quite how much!

So one ventures forth and does it again, carefully, yet whole-heartedly.

One tries again with in the hope that this time it will be ok, this time things will not end the way they did the first time, the time one got so badly hurt through no fault but one's own.

I too hope against hope that this will preferably not end. I dream the dream that millions of Other Women around the world have dreamed across all cultures and centuries. The dream that one day we will have our own personal happy end complete with "and then they lived happily (and together) ever after."

Experience and logic tells me that this is not a very likely outcome, and that it's more likely to end in tears all round yet again.

However, the fact that it happened to me again has shown me that this book wants to be finished, because I keep having to make myself take my own advice....

If I did not know it for certain before learning that Carl, wonderful, vivacious Carl, with all his plans, hopes and dreams, had died, I certainly know it now:

Life is much too short and far too precious to be making bad memories, so please, whatever you do, and however you decide at each junction of your very own journey, make sure that you make memories that count. They could, one day, be all you are left with.

No matter how your own relationship with a married man pans out in the end, I wish you, with all my heart, that one day you look back at it with the same love and affection that I look back on Carl and myself, and that you can say with absolute conviction:

"Yes, it was worth it!"

-2-

How to be the perfect Other Woman in 1 word or 5

In one word:

DON'T

Or in five:

Don't even think about it!

*U*nfortunately chances are that you are not reading this book for the hell of it, or have bought it to be prominently displayed on the shelf between "Knitting for Those with Two Left Hands" and "Korean Art of the 17th Century" because you have a peculiar foible for weird non-fiction books.

If you are reading this book you are probably already past the stage where a simple "Don't do it" will be of any use to you, because you're already right in the middle of a journey that will probably end in tears (mostly and mainly yours).

So rather than waving a warning finger let us see how we can make sure that when you reach your destination (wherever that may be) you and all those that are, and will become, embroiled in it along the route remain relatively unscathed, if at all possible.

Still, there is really no such thing as "The Perfect Other Woman." We can and obviously should try and make the best out of the situation, and we should certainly try and enjoy it while it lasts.

But let us never forget that when we peel away the layers of attraction and emotion and whatever else we bestow upon this relationship, it is, by definition, "wrong" to have an affair with a married man.

Most of us justify what we are doing, by telling ourselves that we are not the ones married to his wife, that it wasn't us who pledged to forsake all others or love her until death do them part.

But when all is said and done we have to accept that no matter how we twist and turn it all in our own minds, we should not have done it.

That does not mean we should walk around beating ourselves up over it, or waste precious time and emotional resources wallowing in pointless puddles of guilt. It just means we should accept the fact and live with it.

- 3 -

The 10 Commandments for the "Perfect Other Woman"

1. You shall guard your heart!

2. You shall not make or rely on too many promises!

3. You shall make no demands!

4. You must not get caught!

5. You shall not get pregnant!

6. You shall know the difference between an affair and a relationship!

7. You shall stay away from his home and family!

8. You shall not whinge, whine, bicker or complain!

9. You shall not force the issue!

10. You shall enjoy it while it lasts!

- 4 -
Things you should not say to the man who is having an affair with you

O nce we have worked out, accepted and finally digested the fundamental truth that what we are engaged in is not a normal relationship we have to accept the facts that it follows different rules and that there are things we should try to refrain from saying and asking if at all possible. It is not easy, but, to be honest, if we had wanted "easy" we would have stayed away from having an affair with a married man in the first place.

So let's have a look at the main words and sentences that should be left unsaid if we want to keep our affair running smoothly:

1) "I love you"

...unless he has said it first in some at least half-credible manner at a time that did not involve any physical activities with one's clothes being partly or fully removed. Unless you want to see just how fast he will turn into the invisible man who has lost your telephone number and drives a 12 mile detour to work every day to avoid coming past your house this is something to keep to yourself if you could not avoid making it a reality in the first place (unwise move).

If he said it and you think he might mean it you need to use your common sense to work out if it is a wise thing to say at that particular time. Chances are it may not be.

By definition two people who really truly love each other should not be having an affair with each other, and once said it can never be un-said. These three words take on a life of their own, they can do damage, they can become threatening and dangerous, and are often the first step on the road to your very own personal Waterloo, one way or the other.

2) "Do you love me?"

That's the dangerous little brother of No 1 (above). Why ask it? The man is married, or at least seriously attached to someone he is supposed to love already. If he does fall in love with you he'll be sure to let you know, when the time is right (which could, of course, be "never"). Depending on how and when you ask chances are you won't believe the answer anyway, especially when answered in an affirmative fashion right in the throws of passion.

When asking a question which can be answered with either a lie or something that will cause hassle and/or arguments one should be aware that the answer is going to be at best unreliable, and at worst something we don't want to hear.

3) The 'leaving wife' question

ANY sentence that combines the words **"your wife"** and **"leaving"** in any way other than "What time is your wife leaving for work?" No, I am absolutely serious. Do not ever, under any circumstances ask, tell or beg him to leave his wife.

You doing so won't actually make him leave his wife, nor will it make him *want* to leave his wife any more than before you uttered the words. It will most likely scare him, irritate him, put him under some amount of pressure (the extent of which will depend on how hardened an adulterer he is) and will do you no good at all. If he brings up the subject then be very careful.

Few married men ever leave their wives for their Other Women, and the small number that actually do are in reverse proportion to the ones that mention the possibility.

Work on the premise that he won't and you'll be quite safe (until the day he suddenly stands in your lounge having done just that, or arrives on your doorstep after she has turfed him out). The whole subject matter of his wife and family is actually best avoided altogether for everyone's peace of mind (such as there is). If you intend to keep having the affair you stay away from any subject that might cause him to run back to the happy home for good if at all possible, and this one is a classic deal-breaker.

4) "But you promised...."

Whatever he promised, and whether he meant it when he did so or not, he was in no position to pledge anything more meaningful to you than not forgetting to put the rubbish out on his way to the car.

We'll look at promises and what they mean in a later chapter, but really and truthfully you knew what his promises are worth when you worked out that he is married (hopefully before he started having an affair with you). His promises to you may well hold as much water as the ones made to his wife. The ones that contained the words "forsaking all others" and "until death do us part." Simple, really, isn't it?

5) "Threats and ultimatums"

Never say "Unless you____ (insert whatever you are trying to get him to do or say) I won't see you any more."

Unless you mean it. If you mean it, well, fine, but in that case you have to follow through. Nothing turns any person, male or female, into a complete doormat more effectively than repeatedly uttering hollow threats.

It's bad enough to be "The Other Woman" – being an "Other Woman" who has "Doormat" written across the forehead is worse. Ultimatums, if you do use them, should only be used for setting a target to yourself. In other words an ultimatum is a tool you can use to give yourself some framework of what is and is not acceptable, with consequences acted upon by yourself if certain targets are not met. But you should not give him an ultimatum if you can avoid doing so, and you should absolutely stick to your ultimatum if you set one.

A complete and utter "No Go" threat is one which ends with the words " ... I will tell your wife about us!" Frankly I really never thought anyone would possibly consider issuing such a threat, until I came across some (thankfully very few) Other Women who actually do or have done so.

That's pure and simple blackmail, and as such it has no place in any relationship, ever.

6) "Honey, guess what, I'm pregnant!"

Obviously! Uttered when not actually true this is a boomerang that will gather force and quite rightly slap you right in the face very hard.

And you will not have been careless / stupid / cunning enough to have managed to get pregnant if you have any last shred of sense or decency, so these words are to be absolutely deleted from your vocabulary forthwith!

7) "Why didn't you call me?"

Why ask such a question (other than to spoil what little time you get to spend together in the first place)? Do you *really* want to hear the answer? Do you *really* want to know that his wife was around him more or less non stop the past few days?

Or that he plain and simply didn't want to call you badly enough to find an excuse to get somewhere where he could? Would either of those answers make you feel any better? And if not, why ask the question? In fact ANY question which you just *know* you won't like the answer to is best left unasked; I mean – what *is* the point?

8) "I would love to meet your kids!"

Urm... why? Even if for some obscure reason you would really want to complicate matters that far – chances are they would not love to meet you, or at least not meet you knowing who you are and what role you are playing in the fate of their family.

Whilst a certain amount of curiosity is only natural, and none of us are completely immune to at least the fleeting fantasy of such a meeting, in real life you should stay away from his family. This is for their protection and for your sanity, and an important enough aspect of having an affair for me to have devoted an entire chapter to it.

Never even contemplate satisfying your curiosity by stalking his children outside school, the playground or via the Internet. Leave them be!

9) "Can't you stay a bit longer?"

If he could *and* wanted to he probably would.

If he doesn't then either he can't or does not want to badly enough, or both. So again, what is the point of asking? In general any question to which there is an obvious answer that might be either untrue or which we would rather not hear is a dumb one to ask.

Don't waste what precious time you have with him on pointless exercises!

10) "Do you still sleep with your wife?"

Do you *really* want to know the answer to that question? And if so; why? They are married (or, in the case of a long term partner, "as good as" married.) They may or may not share a room, a bed and exchange bodily fluids. Whether they do or not is really quite frankly none of your business.

If you get an answer at all it may or may not be the truth, you may or may not believe it, and the question itself will not make the rest of your conversation any more cheerful. So don't ask it. In fact put the question out of your mind completely, anything else comes close to mental masochism.

The happiest "Other Woman" has an ability to blank certain thoughts from her mind, such as whether or not he still sleeps with his wife. This ability also comes in most handy at times such as Christmas, when the image of her beloved, surrounded by his wife and family, singing carols under the Christmas tree, tries to creep up on her conscious mind.

If she can stop these thoughts, or at least push them to the very edge of her consciousness, she will cope much better.

And it is something you can learn, I *know* you can learn it because I myself have managed to do so.

11) "I want more than this affair!"

Oh dear. If you are planning on saying this you had better be fully aware of the consequences.

Once said your "relationship" (such as it is) will probably never be quite the same again. When you got involved with him you knew he was not free. You should have known that what was on offer was "an affair." Don't try and argue with that point, because had anything else been on offer that would have involved an end of the "primary relationship" before entering into the relationship with you.

Of course almost every mistress at least occasionally daydreams about making the transition from "mistress" to "wife / partner," but I'm afraid this is not your call, it is his.

He is the one who is already committed elsewhere. Once you utter those words you will either get lied to, scare him away completely, be given a rather flexible timeline in which such a transition might be possible or not get any meaningful answer at all.

Another problem caused by such a demand is that he may actually suggest that at some point in the future he might contemplate upgrading your status, by means of separation or divorce.

He may even mean it at the time he says it, but in your mind such a conversation plants the seed for expectations, which later grow into demands, and frankly even if you were quite happy with the status quo previously, you will get increasingly less happy as time goes by without anything happening.

12) "Am I prettier / more intelligent / better in bed / whatever / than your wife?"

Another No-Brainer. What do you want to hear? Or rather: What do expect him to reply? You will probably get a "Yes, dear, of course you are…" which will be muttered with a greater or lesser degree of conviction.

And if he has a shred of sensitivity he will wonder why you are so insecure. His wife is nothing to do with you, and it should have no bearing on your well-being or self-esteem whether she is an Angelina Jolie clone or has a PHD in Astrophysics. He is there with you now and that'll have to do you (for now or for as long as it lasts).

13) "Where is this relationship going?"

Yes, everyone appreciates that the Other Woman has an urge to find out the answer to that question at some point. Unfortunately it is such a loaded question, and there really isn't a definite answer to it, the man is married, and unless he has stated otherwise in a halfway credible manner intends to stay married for the time being.

So asking a question which you know will make him uncomfortable, because he either doesn't actually even know the answer, or doesn't think you'll like the answer, or that you know the answer already if you are honest to yourself, is yet another way to spoil a precious and potentially nice evening, and will really and truthfully do no good at all.

At best you'll get some non-committal line that isn't going to help, at worst you'll be lied to and probably know it too.

14) "We have to talk about "us"!"

That is one of the sentences most likely to make almost any man in any type of relationship, from friendship, over fling to full blown affair, and in a "proper" relationship, head for the hills until your urge to "talk about us" has passed.

Basically what it means is "I am going to complain and/or ask you uncomfortable questions." Don't bother – if there is something you want to and need to discuss, and it's not one of the above, just tell him in a perfectly normal way.

Announcing your intention of having a talk will put him in the defensive if he is already there, and bring up urgent reasons why he can't make that date / meeting if he's not.

The problem is that we tend to enter an affair quite with a fairly level head and a healthy degree of realism. Then we find ourselves sucked deeper and deeper emotionally, until we realize that what we bought into with our eyes wide open isn't actually what we are involved in now.

That is the point when we start to want to know "where this is going" and "what we really mean to him."

Unfortunately men hate "let's talk about us" conversations at the best of times, and men who are actually committed elsewhere can't really contribute too meaningfully to such a conversation without lying or feeling under pressure or both.

If we absolutely have to have them they should at least be wrapped into "normal" conversations if at all possible, and not allowed to ruin what precious little time we have together anyway.

The most meaningful conversations of this sort are initiated by him. Waiting for him to bring up the subject matter is therefore a wise move!

- 5 -

Facing facts and quitting excuses

T ime to look at a few home-truths I'm afraid.
Let us assume that you are reading this book because it affects you rather than out of a sense of purely academic curiosity.

So... You are, or have been, or are seriously contemplating doing something that is plain wrong. There is no way to skirt around that particular fact – getting involved with a man who is married or committed to another woman is a pretty damn shabby thing to do whatever the circumstances.

I hope for your sake that you have not complicated the issue even further and maximized the moral indefensibility of the whole mess by picking a man who rightfully belongs to a friend or family member; if you have, well, good luck to you because you're seriously going to need it.

Once you have accepted that what you are doing is basically wrong, is, to a degree, shabby, and will end in tears (most likely, but probably not exclusively, YOURS) it actually gets easier and you are more likely to come out of it with not much worse than a broken heart (which is, lets face it, rarely if ever fatal).

And whilst we are on the subject of facing facts we might as well look at some of the other facts that you will have to learn to accept. When I say "accept" then this means that you face them, you think about them and you make yourself accept them without any "but" 's or the old chestnut "But this is different." There is no such thing as "different" when it comes to affairs, or at least none that could really be (ab)used as a credible excuse, or even carries sufficient weight to serve as an explanation.

Trust me on this one – it may make you feel temporarily better to con yourself into thinking that what you are doing is in some peculiar, miraculous way "different" and therefore somehow more acceptable or less morally indefensible – it's complete nonsense.

An Affair is an Affair is an Affair. And an Affair is, by definition, each and every time, and under all possibly conceivable circumstances, wrong.

That's the way it is and no amount of romantic "soft-focus" or lyrical waxing about it will, in any way, shape or form, alter this fundamental truth.

But, we are doing it anyway and the sooner we come to terms with accepting the fact that we are voluntarily doing something wrong, the sooner we can enjoy it while it lasts. And we might as well enjoy it because the price we are paying is high.

There is a price to pay for everything in life; the price for this episode in ours is likely to be high and pay-day will catch up with us at some stage.

We had better be prepared for it because otherwise it will hit us firmly between the eyes when we least expect it.

Once we have practiced accepting that we are doing something that almost everyone, probably including ourselves, consider to be wrong we can swiftly move on to the next bit of unpalatable truth.

This is the bit where I have to tell you (not that you don't already know it somewhere deep down) that statistically he is probably most unlikely to leave his wife or partner for you.

Please don't gasp, cringe or throw this book into the nearest corner, I promise we'll get on to the more enjoyable aspects of the whole issue soon, but there are a few things that have to be said, digested and accepted before we can move on.

Only a relatively small percentage of unfaithful men leave their wife for their Other Woman, and whilst we're on that subject I can't spare you the old saying "When a man marries his mistress he creates a vacancy." Think about that one too.

If your sole or main reason for being and staying involved with this man is the hope that one day he will leave his wife, get a divorce, and become your full-time partner, you should seriously consider getting out while you still can.

You would do well to work on the premise that you are the Other Woman, she is the wife (or long term partner), and that this is how it will stay for the foreseeable future.

Then look the most likely long term outcome squarely in the eye: His wife will still be his wife and you will still be The Other Woman in years to come; or, you will no longer be his Other Woman, replaced by either A.N.Other or a period of monogamous behavior on his part.

One of the things that surprised me most when I researched this book was just how many women were involved with married men for very long periods of time. I had originally, naively, assumed that after a year, maybe two at most, these things resolve themselves or end. The fact that so many women are still hiding in the shadows of a man's life after 5, 10 and even over 20 years with no end in sight, honestly amazed me.

When we do something we KNOW to be wrong we appear to have an illogical but nevertheless deep-rooted desire to find "explanations" (I will be brutal and honest enough to call them by their real name: Excuses) to somehow justify what we do.

This is, to an extent, understandable when we speak to 3rd parties as it does not tend to feel particularly good to say "Well, I am a morally degenerate person and I am having an affair with this man because I don't give a damn about who gets hurt and what havoc it will wreak with whoever's lives" - even if this were, to a greater or lesser extent, actually not as far from the truth as we like to believe.

We all feel a need to like ourselves, and whilst we will expect and partly even tolerate the fact that the above (worded similarly or worse depending on who says or thinks it in which company) is expressed by others, we do tend to try and manipulate the naked truth by decorating it with feelings, emotions, explanations and even downright lies. Not just towards others, but towards ourselves as well.

But to truly cope with having an affair we have to be honest, at least with ourselves, and once again I will feed you a few home-truths....

So, let's look at some of the most common attempts to justify, explain and excuse what we are doing:

• **"I could not help it"** (accompanied by batting of eyelashes, moist eyes, and followed or preceded by either a deep sigh or a sob for added effect)

Well, sorry, BUT: Pull the other one. There are very few things in life where "I could not help it" is a valid explanation for allowing something to happen. Being struck by lightning comes closer (although even then it could be argued that one could have stayed out of harm's way) – getting hit by a bus may qualify, or catching a cold.

But no way on God's earth does this wash in connection with having an affair with a married / attached man. Don't say "but..." – You know it, I know it, and everyone else with an IQ in excess of their shoe-size knows it too.

You COULD have helped it, just as I could have helped it, had we WANTED to.

What, for some reason or the other, and these

reasons will vary from situation to situation, we appear to be unable to do is WANT to "help it." Think about it. There is a difference....

Do yourself a favor, don't use that one any more, casting yourself in the role of the helpless victim of some all-encompassing force beyond your control may dull the feelings of guilt to an extent but one can only lie to oneself for so long before one ends up seeing the liar as well as the cheater staring back in the mirror.

.
• **"But I fell in LOVE"** (same moist eyes and sob / sigh routine as before, or both for good measure.)

Yes. OK. So maybe you did. I did too. But do you know what? It doesn't actually matter, it is no excuse, and it's a poor explanation. If you are quite honest you probably went "that step too far" before you fell in love anyway. In many ways it makes it worse, especially for you. You may or may not know how right I am in that particular respect at this point; if you don't (yet), you will in due course.

Now we move on swiftly to my personal favorite

• **"It just HAPPENED!"** (Depending on one's individual make-up accompanied by the "sob/s sigh/moist eye" thing, or a simple shrug from a more hardened individual.)

Oh PLEASE! These things absolutely, categorically and truly do not "just happen." We either positively, actively *make* them happen, or we passively *let* them happen, or, usually, a combination of the two.

But people do not start an affair by some miraculous process of molecular osmosis which transported them into each other's arms without any prior warning and entirely without their knowledge or consent.

Usually there is a point of no return, a line which is crossed and after which things actually do tend to take on a life of their own.

But we see this line quite clearly. Whether we cross it or not is a matter of choice, not something that "just happens." As we approach "the line" we may kid ourselves that we won't cross it, that we are just going to the edge to take a look and indulge in a little game of "What if....?" However, the fact of the matter is that deep down we have probably, if not almost certainly, decided to cross the line should the opportunity present itself by the time we recognize it, long before we actually reach it.

• **"But it's DIFFERENT with us...."** No, dear, sorry. It isn't, actually.

Or at least it is no more or no less different than any other affair ever started, conducted or ending in tears throughout the rather long history of mankind. Believe it, ignore it, cope with it – whatever.

Having an affair is wrong. Call it "different" if it makes you feel any better (why?), but don't kid yourself into using it as an excuse.

In fact you'd do well to just quit the excuses and explanations altogether. Just do what you have to do and accept that you're doing so.

Your excuses / explanations won't wash with those that are wronged in all this, and whilst you may well find one or the other well-meaning friend who may sit and nod semi-sympathetically as you tell them, it won't really truly wash with them either.

What I am trying to get across with those examples (and they are just a few), is that we may lie to others as to why we are having an affair with a man we should not be touching with a bargepole, but we should at least be honest with ourselves.

So now I have reminded you why you did NOT start your affair, let's have a look at some of the reasons why normally perfectly "nice" girls cross the line and become "The Other Woman."

Why do women REALLY have affairs with married / attached / otherwise unavailable men? And why do they find it so hard to admit the real reasons to anyone, including or even especially to themselves?

To be brutally honest the most common situations that lead down the slippery path from an innocent look that lasts just a little longer than strictly necessary to finding oneself in the starring role of one's very own sordid affair are, more often than not, disappointingly mundane.

We spin a web of deceit and try to justify it by wrapping it into notions of great romance and endless love, spiced up with a hefty dose of irresistible passion. We wrap the affair into imaginative tales of star struck lovers akin to Romeo and Juliet in our own heads whilst pressing the replay button of "meaningful songs." I admit, with some trepidation, to having literally worn out CDs from Celine Dion to Sting and back via Bill Withers, Coldplay and anything that contained a shred of lyrics I could apply to my situation.

We daydream, and those little private movies that run riot in our minds cast us in the role of the tragic heroine, not the wicked witch that steals a man and single-handedly destroys a happy family.

The truth, of course, as always, tends to lie somewhere in between, but it is human nature not to want to view one's own actions in the coldest light of realism. And frankly that's OK, as long as we don't completely lose touch with the facts and drift away on a pink cloud of romantic drivel.

Affairs happen for a variety of reasons, but most tend to be born out of a fairly simple constellation which involves a man, a woman, a dose of boredom, a sprinkling of curiosity, a pinch (or a shovel) of sexual attraction and a sense of adventure.

Add to that the discovery of common grounds, shared views, interests, and a connection of minds.

Set this potentially explosive recipe in the right place at the right time in two people's lives, and watch the birth of yet another affair.

Feelings usually come into it - of course they do, but more often than not they just complicate the issue at a later date, when the whole drama has already moved into the "full blow affair" mode, rather than being the actual cause of it. Couples tend to think the feelings were the root cause and only see in hindsight that this is only partly correct.

This is something that women find particularly hard to admit, we do not enjoy seeing ourselves as people who recklessly risk causing hurt and wreaking havoc for no "good reason."

So by subconsciously inventing "good reasons" why we are having an affair we move away from the mental image of a bunny-boiling Glen Close in "Fatal Attraction" towards one that is much kinder on the conscience. To a degree this is fine. We all have to live with what we do in some way or the other. Just always try and keep a grip on these notions; they serve their purpose as a coping mechanism, but must not be allowed to take on a life of their own.

Another aspect is firmly anchored in the old belief that women don't have sex for the sake of having sex. Society accepts (more or less cheerfully) that this is something men do, but the idea of a woman doing the same elicits a minimum of raised eyebrows.

So women tend to wrap sexual desire into feelings (real or imagined) and emotional fairy-tales to be able to allow themselves to enter a sexual relationship, even without the added "shock-horror" scenario of the object of their desire being otherwise attached.

Lastly women frequently have affairs because consciously or subconsciously they do not actually want a relationship that follows the more conventional rules. They pick a man they can't have fully so they don't actually HAVE to have him full time. Again this is not the thing that nice little girls are brought up to have on their agenda, so it is not admitted to readily.

A very good friend of mine fairly recently confessed that whilst she "sort of" wanted a relationship, someone to hold her, someone to make love with, laugh with, have fun with, she did not actually have the time for a "proper" relationship with all bells and whistles attached.

We idly discussed that dilemma over a glass of wine or two without really coming to any satisfactory conclusion for a while before moving on to more interesting subjects.

And low and behold, not two weeks later she had met a man who fitted into her life perfectly, because he was married, intended to stay that way, and lived a safe 50-odd mile away.

The proof of this particular pudding is the considerable percentage of mistresses who, after weeks / months or even years of allegedly wanting to have the man all for themselves, run screaming the other way when he actually stands on their doorstep (complete with a week's worth of dirty washing) with the immortal words "I have left her" on his lips.

Having an affair with a married man can actually be a very convenient (sorry, I know that sounds quite dreadfully callous but it's no less true for it) way for a woman to have her cake and eat it too.

For the woman who, deep down, does not want a full-time committed conventional relationship at a specific stage of her life, yet does not want to be completely without some of the more positive aspects of having a man around some of time, an affair can be just what suits her.

As more and more women have successful careers and do not have to rely on a man to provide a roof over her head and food on the table this particular scenario will be on the increase rather than otherwise.

- 6 -

Anatomy of Adultery

Adultery comes in many forms. And just as varied are people's definitions as to what constitutes "cheating." Whilst some people call a close friendship between a married man and a female more than questionable, others define "being unfaithful" only as having actual sexual intercourse with a third party.

Then there are variations on the theme. Some class a kiss on the lips as unacceptable behavior for a married person, others define unfaithfulness less in physical, and more in emotional terms and include the sharing of confidences in the overall category of "being unfaithful."

In this day and age there are various forms of relationships that never get physically consummated, but are, by some definition, classed as affairs or adultery, such as what happens on countless forums and via e-mail and chat all over the world.

People have left their spouse and moved across the world for someone they have never even met in real life. The Internet has become a platform for emotionally charged relationships that are no less consuming than those acted out in real life.

I have one very close friend who built up an online friendship with a married man over several months, and within a week of actually meeting up for the first time in real life they had both left their wife and husband respectively, and were moving in together.

They have now been married for a number of years and have the happiest marriage of all the people I know except maybe for my former in-laws.

The main forms of real life, nitty gritty adultery however are divided into three main categories, or four if you include the non-sexual overly close emotional attachment that some married people have with a special friend (which, perhaps oddly, many find more threatening and/or potentially upsetting than a less intense, yet sexual encounter).

1)   The One-Night Stand
2)   The Fling
3)   The Affair

The One Night Stand

The One Night Stand is, contrary to popular belief, not necessarily a one-time-only event. It is entirely possible for a married man to have multiple one night stands with the same person without it actually being classified as an affair.

One Night Stands are defined by their lack of lasting (!) emotional attachment. There is usually no real promise to carry on past dawn (and if there is one it's generally not kept) and realistically do little or no real harm to a marriage if they remain secret.

Frankly men who admit a One Night Stand to their wife without any pressing need (such as the lady in question turning out to be a deranged Bunny-Boiler seriously threatening to blow the whistle on him, or him being stupid enough to have got her pregnant or having caught some STD) are idiots, or men who wanted to destroy their marriage for some reason quite unconnected to the One Night Stand anyway.

One Night Stands are by far the least dangerous form of infidelity. In fact they are less of a threat to a marriage than a close, yet entirely platonic, friendship with a member of the opposite sex. They are just sex, and have no lasting effect on either participant than being another memory to recall in old age when thinking back upon "the wild years." One Night Stands only become a problem or a threat if either participant changes the goalpost, if due caution was not exercised or when it is discovered. Sometimes the conscience plays tricks on the married man, which can cause some anguish or even lead to the very unwise decision to confess all, but generally a One Night Stand is, in the overall scheme of adultery, a harmless interlude.

The Fling

A fling may or may not turn into an affair, but in itself, and during its duration (i.e. before it either ends or turns into an affair) it is defined by the fact that it is not meant to last.

There may be a degree of emotional attachment, but the main difference between a fling and an affair is that it has an anticipated, and agreed to, end, and that it does not try to be or copy a relationship.

Flings are like exotic holidays. They are to be enjoyed for what they are, an escape from normal life, something wonderful and something that will be terminated at a defined point with a sense of regret that it's over, but no bitter feelings.

Just as we return to normal life after a holiday, with great memories, and a bit of sadness that it didn't go on longer, we can return to "life as we know it" after a fling relatively or entirely unscathed, with nothing more than a set of fabulous memories and no emotional wounds to turn into scars.

Just like people tend to wonder fleetingly what it would be like to give up their normal life and emigrate to their holiday destination, you and the married man you are having a fling with may idly let their imagination run riot with thoughts of "what if....?" – but just like holiday makers get onto the plane after their stay and return home your fling will reach its (almost inevitable) conclusion with little or no ill-effect on all concerned.

If you are having a fling, enjoy it. Make happy memories to revisit in your mind like a favorite beach, and move on after it has reached its end. It was a fling. It was great. It is over. Get it?

The Affair

The main difference between an affair and either a friendship, a Fling or a One Night Stand is that it is defined by a greater or lesser degree of emotional attachment and the fact that it does not have an anticipated and agreed end.

Whilst the anticipated and agreed to end of a One Night Stand is the hastily consumed cup of coffee before returning to life as we know it, and the Fling is accepted to last a few days, sometimes weeks, an affair does not have an anticipated or agreed on end.

Or at least not an end that is worked into the equation at the time of it becoming clear that there is an affair happening.

An affair is closest in its nature to a committed relationship, with many of the dynamics being the same or similar. The fact that there are no generally acknowledged rules to speak of means that relationship rules are usually applied.

Obviously we seldom really know quite what we are getting ourselves into at the start, and the borderline between where a friendship ends and an affair begins can be fluid and open to interpretation.

Some affairs are born out of friendships, some developed from a One Night Stand. Sometimes an emotionally attachment leads to a fully fledged affair, and sometimes a sexual attraction eventually grows into a deep love.

There *is* no such thing as "a typical affair" when we look at each situation more closely.

- 7 -

Prerequisites for having an affair

*H*aving an affair is not for everyone.... Now obviously we all know that we should not be having an affair anyway. It's wrong, ok?

But certain types of people are more likely to have an affair without making themselves (and others) deeply unhappy, and without having it affect their life too negatively.

Most women who have an affair with a married man *will* actually be deeply unhappy at times, and will cry many a tear they could have avoided shedding had they not got involved with a married man. But some types are more likely than others to come out the other end relatively unscathed, and more likely to find some real happiness with their married partner than others.

The woman most likely to have a successful affair (for want of a better turn of phrase) is basically happy, both with herself and her life as a whole, of an independent nature, with a full life, hobbies of her own, and, very importantly, a really good supportive set of friends, preferably friends who don't know her lover at all, or at least not too well.

She may have fallen into her affair more or less by accident, while she was not actively seeking a relationship. She is most likely quite busy with work, her hobbies, her friends and one or two time- and energy-consuming pursuits.

This means she will find the unavoidable restrictions and disadvantages that having an affair inflicts upon her far more bearable. She will not have too much spare time or emotional energy to dwell on the downsides of being a mistress, and if her lover cancels an eagerly anticipated evening with her at the last minute it will not throw her into unbearable turmoil.

In other words, her lover will be a part of her life. Maybe the most important part, maybe the part she is most passionate about, but the gap he would leave if he was suddenly gone would not mean that there was very little left in her life because he and the affair had filled almost her entire existence.

A woman like that, hopefully blessed with a varied set of friends both male and female, will be upset at times when things don't go her way, will miss him when she can't see him as much as she would like to (as will be the case in most affairs), but it won't cause her to slide into any form of near-terminal decline.

Friends are a vital factor in successfully surviving an affair anyway. Friends to go out with, friends to talk to, friends to inject a dose of much needed realism from time to time. Friends to hug, friends to fix the dripping tap, pick her up when the car breaks down, friends to be a shoulder to cry on and friends to just be, well, friends.

In some ways friends will have to take on many of the functions a full time, "conventional" partner normally would. Having an affair means the one person we probably most want to have by our side, in our arms or on the other end of the phone during life's little and large disasters will not be available to us at the times we want and need them most.

Personally I find my male friends invaluable, to the extent that one of them, only half jokingly, accused me of having dismembered a "normal" relationship and having dished out the various roles that usually a partner takes on amongst a few carefully selected male friends. I laughed at that notion at first, then had to admit that subconsciously (yet rather effectively if I say so myself), I may have done just that.

Girlfriends are, as always, incredibly important, and the happiest Other Women have a selected and small number of female friends who know about their affair and are, if not precisely thrilled or approving, at least reasonably or wholly supportive. Obviously we have to be both careful and selective in whom we tell, and female friends who know the married lover's wife must not be told, however trustworthy they may seem at the time of being confided in.

Unhappily married friends are best spared details of one's affair, as are women who have found out that their own husbands (ex or current) have been unfaithful, especially if their own marriage was destroyed by that and if they are still cut up about that.

They are most unlikely to lend a sympathetic ear to a woman who is doing to a wife what was done to them. (And no, those women are absolutely *not* the ones to have the "But his wife is not my responsibility" conversation with, however tempting that may be at times!)

Women who should avoid having an affair at all cost, and who should, for the sake of their sanity and long term happiness, seriously consider getting out of the one they have if they are already involved with a married man, are those who are basically lonely and who have little else to concentrate on in their life than the man they are seeing.

Tragically there are all too many women who entered into an affair as strong capable and busy ladies with a large circle of friends, a great career, and a number of hobbies, and who have, as a result of the affair, let many of these important aspects of their lives slide. So they started out as the kind of woman most likely to survive having an affair relatively unscathed, even enjoying it, and turned into the kind of woman who really should not be in an affair as it is doing them far more harm than it brings enjoyment.

The danger is that as women we tend to want to accommodate, so many women unfortunately try and be available at all times in case their married lover could want to see them. They avoid making arrangements to see friends, don't plan regular evenings out any longer, let their hobbies and interests slide and neglect to keep in touch with their friends and acquaintances. The result of that sort of behavior is increasing isolation which leads to the married man taking on an even greater part of the woman's life, and so the vicious circle continues to spiral downwards.

Those are then the women who are most likely to get clingy, to start pushing him to leave his wife, or to begin behaving in a manner that will not make him want to spend increasing amounts of time with her fairly swiftly.

It is vitally important to always remember that the man we are involved with is married, and that he is cheating on his wife with us because there is something (or hopefully "many things") about us that makes him want to be with us. That is the pleasant part of the equation.

The other bit is that he is with us because there are aspects about his marriage and the way he and his wife interact with each other, that are far from perfect.

The easiest way to make him run a mile, either back to the happy home or straight into the arms of another, new, mistress, is to replicate one too many of the negative aspects of his marriage or main relationship.

We need to be quite clear about it in our own heads: A mistress is more easily replaced or terminated than a wife. So by behaving in such a way that he does not *want* to be with us any more we are heading with breakneck speed for the status of "ex-mistress."

Another character trait that is likely to lead to a very unhappy (and probably short-lived) affair is excessive jealousy. In fact the less jealous a mistress is by nature the more likely she is to have an affair that gives her joy.

Jealousy is (in my humble opinion, speaking as someone whose is very luckily not afflicted by the green eyed monster at all) an unpleasant and destructive state of mind at the best of times, and in an affair it is probably fatal. Fatal either to the affair itself, or the sanity of the jealous mistress, or, most likely, sooner or later, both.

It's a No-Brainer, really.... The man you are having an affair with is having another relationship. He is married. He has a wife. He is probably (whatever he may or may not be telling you) still sleeping with his wife at least occasionally. I personally do not ask, do not want to know, and immediately stop any conversation heading for the subject dead in its tracks.

He is almost certainly hugging her, kissing her, discussing things of importance with her. He is waking up next to her, having his coffee with her in the morning and is going back to her sooner or later in the evening.

And the worst thing is, we have no *right* to be jealous of her. She is his wife for crying out loud, so everything he does with her is as it should be, and it's *us* who are the intruders in the whole setup, so nothing is quite as displaced as jealousy. Unfortunately in my experience jealous people may be able to control how they act on their jealous feelings, but they rarely manage to actually control the jealousy itself. So they will, sooner or later, either make themselves exceptionally unhappy, or cause him infinite hassle, or both.

The mental picture of "him" in bed with his wife, his arm wrapped around her waist, her face turned to him, whilst we are tossing and turning in our beds trying to find some sleep, is not going to be a pleasant one at the best of time. It takes a great deal of self control to ward off images like that, and if you tend to be consumed by jealousy at much lesser thoughts you're in for a pretty rough ride.

Jealousy is also a very bad emotion to be afflicted with when serious decisions need to be taken, or when the inevitable thoughts of doing something crassly stupid such as forcing the issue or, god forbid, the temptation to let the wife know once and for all what's going on, raise their ugly heads.

So if you are the jealous type – control yourself, (yes you can) or leave having affairs to those who can handle it.

Remember that a jealous mistress is a troublesome mistress. A jealous mistress is hassle. Hassle is not what a man has an affair for; hassle is what his affair is supposed to take him away from! An overly jealous mistress is also a dangerous one, and he will see displays of excessive jealousy as a warning sign if he has any sense at all.

Personally I am glad that I am not the jealous type, and yet, even as a non-jealous person I very carefully avoid the subject, and do not allow myself to think of him with his wife. Thoughts of the possibility of him sharing intimate moments (of an emotional, intellectual or obviously sexual nature) with a third person are even worse. After all, his wife *is* his wife and we knew this before we got involved, but a secondary mistress would be taking things a step too far even for non-jealous me.

To be happy in a relationship with a married man we have to be absolutely clear about the fact that we are, for all intents and purposes, leading the life of a single woman, but with some of the benefits and restrictions of being in a relationship.

This means we are responsible for our day-to-day life, and our happiness, largely ourselves.

It therefore follows that we should, right at the outset, get used to the idea that we can not rely on a man to be there for us the same way a husband (well, a husband married to us rather than someone else) would.

Once we get that bit of reality firmly embedded into our brain we can move on building the kind of life that allows "real life" and "the affair" to exist happily side by side.

By having a happy and joyful life outside the affair we will be a happier and "fun to be with" affair partner, and having a happy affair will benefit us in the other aspects of our lives, so if we can manage the admittedly difficult balancing act of weaving everything into the fabric of our life without letting the affair take it over, we should, in theory, be equipped to handle things.

It is absolutely fatal (sooner or later) to allow ourselves to become a needy, clingy, whining Other Woman who picks an argument or complains or cries about the state of the affair almost every time she sees her married partner.

There is no more surefire method to make him want to see less of us or even finish the affair completely than to behave in a way that makes us no fun to be with more often than not.

He is having an affair because things aren't going well in his marriage. So when things are going just as badly in his affair there is really and truthfully very little reason to carry on the affair.

One of the worst things that can ever be said to an Other Woman is "You are behaving just like my wife!" Think about it, what in heaven's name would make a half-reasonable man want to be with, let alone leave his wife for, a woman who is displaying the very characteristics which, displayed at the home front, caused him to have an affair in the first place.

- 8 -
Why he is having an affair

*T*here are as many real reasons why a married man may end up having an affair with you as there are married men having affairs.

However, these highly individual reasons tend to fall into one of a rather more restricted number of categories, and it is these basic categories that we will have a closer look at in this chapter.

Obviously you will want to believe that he is with you because you are so irresistible, because he fell head over heels in love with you, because you and him are true soul mates, are the reinvention of Romeo and Juliet and whatever else we all tend to try and kid ourselves into believing.

But the truth of the matter, unpalatable as it may be, is that the real reasons why this man is cheating on his wife with you are generally far more mundane, and not always what we would like to hear at all.

Even if your affair has turned a corner and become something "much more" (whatever that may be and however much most people, at some point, believe their affair to be "much more"), the way it started out was probably still according to one of the main categories of adultery.

Generally men cheat on their wives for a reason that falls into one of three main categories.

They may either still love their wife but there is something seriously missing from their relationship, they may no longer love their wife sufficiently to stay faithful so cheat on her, or they may cheat because they can and will do so whether they love their wife or not.

Men who fall into the last category are best avoided completely, but sadly you don't tend to find out until it's too late unless they are exceedingly honest as well as habitually and/or naturally unfaithful. These men will not be any more faithful to you than they are to their current wife, and if they cheat purely for sport and for the sake of cheating then they may very well lie for the sake of lying and treat you badly for the sake of it as well.

However, men that fall into that third category usually tend to concentrate on quick conquests and short flings, rather than letting themselves in for affairs, so we need not look at them too closely anyway.

Men who love their wives and yet cheat on them are difficult to deal with simply because they tend to feel far guiltier about what they are doing than those who no longer love their wife enough to stay faithful, which does not make them the most entertaining company.

The obvious question in their case is "So if you love your wife, what on earth are you doing sleeping with me?"

Try not to actually ask that question, he will probably be unable to offer you (or, for that matter, himself) a really satisfactory answer anyway.

So why *do* men who love their wife have affairs?

Well, for the same reasons any man has an affair, and the really flippant answer tends to be

"Because they can."

or

"Few men need a reason, most just need an opportunity. "

It is nowhere near as simple as (just) that of course. Humans in general do things because of a mixture of need and opportunity.

If I am hungry and there is food I will eat it. Now I may be on a diet or follow some specific eating plan, so I may stick to the food I am allowed at the times I am allowed it, but basically if I am hungry enough, have not had the chance to eat what I wanted or needed for long enough, have no overwhelmingly compelling reason not to eat, and there is a piece of Black Forest cake throwing itself at my mouth at just the right moment I may well eat it.

To spin that analogy further – if at home I have all the food I could possibly want, and the ability and opportunity to eat it when and how I like, I am much more likely to not even notice a piece of Black Forest cake, however tempting, or I may notice it and appreciate it for the fine piece of German bakery art that it is, but I won't eat it or even really want to eat it.

A happily married man who is in a fulfilling relationship with his wife will not usually have an affair. He may, if several factors play together, have a One Night Stand or even a fling, but rarely an affair. Frankly why should he?

Basically a man will have an affair when some other woman offers, or appears to offer, things he is not getting in or from his marriage. These "things" are as varied as the men who need them, they could include sex, or intimacy, or closeness. All three more often than not, actually.

Someone who listens to him, someone who takes him seriously. Admires him, thinks he is funny, great looking, intelligent and generally wonderful (never underestimate the male ego and its needs).

It could also be argued, and is, in fact, argued by as many scientists as it is refuted by others, that the human male is simply not designed to be monogamous.

That he is genetically and by evolution designed to "go forth and multiply." The argument whether this is the case or not has been raging for a long time, I have no idea if it is true or just a lame excuse, so won't go on about it without any real evidence to support it validity one way or the other.

Also, whilst being true would explain why humans change their partner during their lifetime, it does not really go a long way to bring us any closer to telling us why they have affairs rather than ending their current relationship first.

To some men having a mistress is also at least partly a lifestyle choice. Almost along with the great home, the successful career, the membership to the right golf-course, and the expense account. It becomes part of their rewards in life for being a "success."

Men who keep a mistress as a status symbol (even if it is a hidden one that only they, themselves and maybe some very close friends know) tend to choose mistresses that are likely to be younger, very attractive, and of a certain "value." Trophy mistresses so to speak, to go with the "trophy wife" they have at home in the "trophy home."

He and his wife may have been on a similar level when they first got married, then he started a successful career, rose up the ranks socially and professionally, while his wife stayed much on the same level for one of a variety of reasons. So suddenly he finds himself in a situation where he (consciously or subconsciously) believes he ought to "trade up" as far as his woman is concerned. He then picks a mistress that appears to be more befitting his actual or perceived status in life.

Also a lifestyle choice, but of another kind, is the one made by the man who has a relationship with another woman to escape from a life that isn't going at all as he would wish.

Possibly trapped in a marriage he would rather not be in but can't seem to get out of, with a career that isn't really going anywhere much either, and quite possibly money problems.

That kind of man finds an escape from his worries in a relationship with a woman who probably doesn't really know the extent or even the existence of his troubles. He may even pretend to be someone quite different when he is with her. He lives the life he would actually like to live, pretends to be the man he would like to be and thinks he should have been. He tends to choose a mistress from outside his usual circle, and often keeps up the pretense for quite a while, if not for the entire duration of the affair. In his case (and probably his case only), the Other Woman is quite right when she says "He turned out to be not the man I thought he was at all" – because, when he was with her actually *wasn't!*

While we are on the subject of things not being what they seem to be, us "Other Women" are often, if not even usually, guilty of projecting all we ever wanted in a man and out of a relationship into our affairs as well.

Because this "relationship" of ours does not have to withstand the test of everyday life, as a general rule, we usually only get to see the best of our married lovers. We can generally be at our best behavior when we see them too. So we can build up and maintain (for a while at least, but sometimes for many years) this great structure which consists of two people showing one another their best sides, keeping the lid on our less adorable features, and living out a part time version of the relationship we would love to have if only life and our inevitable imperfections didn't get in the way.

However, back to the many varied reasons why a man may be having an affair with you – the greatest facilitator of affairs is simply opportunity.

Given the right woman at the right time, the right state of mind and a strong dose of chemistry, many a man who would, just weeks previously, have sworn that he was entirely faithful, will end up on the slippery slope to a fully blown affair, or at least have a One Night Stand.

Another often ignored path to the slippery slope is friendship. A man and a woman who have possibly been friends for years, and suddenly find their friendship changing.

A purely platonic friendship between a man and a woman is obviously entirely possible, but quite often one or the other develops feelings for the friend which are crossing the border between purely platonic and attraction of a different kind.

When close friendships turn into affairs the potential for long term hurt is almost greater than in any other affair, because one does not just risk having one's heart broken, but risks losing a great friendship as well because there is usually absolutely no way back to the friendship as it was once the line has been crossed. The road from friendship to affair is usually a one-way only one, and more often than not a dead-end road as well.

- 9 -
Types of men to avoid at all cost

If you can....

It may be too late for you to follow the advice in this chapter at the moment, as you may well be already involved with a man that falls into one, or, god help you, more than one of the categories mentioned.

But even if that is the case, it may inject a little dose of reality to your consciousness, and maybe you will remember it in the future, just at a time when you still have a say in the matter, just before you reach the famous point of no return.

Obviously the main type of man to avoid is the one with a ring on his finger, or a ring that should be on his finger if he were to wear it.

In other words, a married man. But as this is a book that concerns itself with affairs with married men we just have to accept that sometimes we will fall for a married man, and simply look at the types of married men that will cause us more trouble than others, and more trouble than they are worth.

For some reason women seem to apply a different set of criteria to their married lovers than they would apply in the choice of a regular partner.

However, the fact of the matter is that the choice of the man we fall in love with has an absolutely irrefutable effect on the likely outcome of the relationship. Choosing wisely (and avoiding the ones who are no good for us and would be no good for us even if they were not married) is the be all and end all of a satisfactory affair. A bad man is a bad man, married or single or divorced or widowed. Frankly starting an affair with a man we would not usually start a relationship with is a good first step towards disaster. A One Night Stand or a Fling, maybe, but if a man would not be good enough for us to have a relationship with then he is not good enough to have an affair with.

A very peculiar and borderline entertaining little bit of food for thought is the fact that when you ask women what they are looking for in a partner, more often than not the words "faithful" and "honest" are pretty high on their list of priorities.

Yet here we are, in love or at least pretty closely involved with men who are, by definition of being with us in the first place, neither honest nor faithful.

They lie to be with us, and they are unfaithful with us.

Just a thought to keep readily at the back of our minds. Not to necessarily dwell on or to make an issue out of, but to be filed away along with other little truths about that man for the future.

Just as very significant number of conventional relationships start at work, so do a large number of affairs. Probably around half if the statistics I have seen, and the comments made to me by the people I have spoken to throughout the time I was researching this book, are anything to go by.

It is always a potential risk to date someone you work with, but if they are not your superior or married, or both, it is generally something that can be worked around, and if the relationship ends it also does not tend to necessarily, or even too often, become a career-threatening event.

If you date a married man you work with, and especially when he is your boss, it becomes a far more dangerous game, the stakes are much higher, and you could easily be gambling with your career and income as well as with your heart.

It also means that work will not provide you with a place to get your mind off things when the affair isn't going quite as swimmingly as you would have hoped. And if, or should I say "when," it ends you are in for a terribly rough ride and one of you could easily be forced to change your job.

When you have an affair with someone who is above you in the company hierarchy and especially if he is your immediate superior, the balance of your relationship is stacked against you from the word go.

Few people manage to separate their personal life from their work as effectively as would be necessary to make an affair with your married boss a healthy relationship. It will affect both your work and your personal life negatively, and when you add the gossip of your co-workers, and the obviously to be expected repercussions should the affair end, you see why this one comes very firmly under the heading "Not a Good Idea."

In many countries companies have more or less strict rules on relationships between co-workers, and some are so strict that a discovered affair will result in instant dismissal for one or both "offenders". This means if you do get involved with a married man at work you should be even more discrete than you must be anyway, or you could suddenly find yourself without a lover and without a job at a time when the loss of either would cause your whole life to take a serious turn for the worse.

Having an affair with someone who is your boss or significantly higher up in the company hierarchy is likely to make for an unhealthy balance in the relationship. Some people manage to separate their affair and their work life to a degree, but those who believe that one does not, in any way, affect the other are probably deluding themselves. The dynamics of the job will usually affect the affair and vice versa, and not usually in a good or healthy way.

The same actually goes for most men who have some kind of influence over you through their profession, and whose professional involvement with you can not be easily ended or transferred.

Customers may be okay, or colleagues from other divisions, preferably other offices.

But your doctor, your therapist, your lawyer and your trainer are probably a bit to close for comfort; your teacher or pupil definitely is.

If you start an affair with one of the above it is not just wise, but imperative that you should terminate their professional involvement with you as soon as you are heading for an affair, or immediately after it has started at the latest.

It is easy enough to find another doctor, lawyer or trainer, and you will stand a better chance of getting what you need out of both the professional and your lover if they are not the same person....

One group of men I feel should be most definitely and absolutely out of bounds are the husbands of close friends (any friends really) and those men married to female members of your family.

Nothing in the world is worth the disaster and heartbreak that is potentially lurking just below the surface of such an affair, and trust me, having an affair with a man who is not married to someone to whom you owe decency, friendship, loyalty and integrity, is hard enough and stretches most women's ability to cope to breaking point at times.

If you have to handle everything that naturally comes with being the Other Woman plus the knowledge that you are betraying someone who probably loves you, and trusts you with all her heart, because you are their friend, or their sister, you may well have a very hard time looking in the mirror at yourself without a degree of contempt.

To find out that one's husband is, or has been having an affair is devastating enough at "the best (?) of times." To find that a relative or close friend was the "Other Woman" will constitute a double betrayal of enormous proportions, and many betrayed wives will actually judge the friend's or relative's betrayal even more harshly than that inflicted upon them by their husbands.

On a more practical and selfish note when your affair with an outsider breaks up you can count on the support of your family and friends, and will (hopefully) know that they will be there to catch you and pick up the pieces.

When you have an affair with the husband of a close friend or family member, and the whole thing goes pearshaped, you will most likely find yourself on the receiving end of repercussions you never imagined possible, and will have to go through them quite alone because the ones you should and normally would be turning to for support are the ones you have betrayed and who are now turning their back on you.

Bridges burnt like that are usually hard (in the case of family) or impossible (in the case of close friends) to rebuild, so please do yourself and those close to you a favor and hunt elsewhere.

The "serial offender," a man who has a string of affairs to his name, is to be avoided unless you are quite all right with being one of a string of women he has affairs with. This kind of man will move on in due course to pastures new, and unless you have a pretty good grip on your own emotions you will be badly hurt when he does. It is hard enough when a man decides to end the affair because he wants to make another go of his marriage, but to find oneself replaced by another "Other Woman" is infinitely harder still.

You may, of course, not find out until it's too late to extricate from the situation without any major heartache, but often the signs were there from the start and we just chose to ignore them. In that respect affairs are no different to other relationships. Hope springs eternal and women have a fatal habit of convincing themselves that, improbable as it may seem, they are the one who will save his soul and change his ways.

But leopards don't change their spots any more than men change their ways that easily once they are set in them.

Going into a relationship of any sort with the declared intention of changing the man involved is at best a futile exercise. In fact I have always thought it to be a sign of arrogance on the part of the woman – what makes us think that we will be the one to succeed where so many others have failed? And why go into a relationship with someone who would require changing into someone else to be suitable in the first place?

So if you see yourself confronted with a man you'd have to change to really want to be with – back away gracefully or accept that he is what he is, enjoy the ride and deal with the consequences as and when they present themselves.

It is obviously possible to have a happy affair with

someone who would have to be changed to be a suitable full-time partner. The very fact that he is not a full time partner means that we can live with whatever would irritate us intensely if we had him around the whole time.

It goes without saying that abusive men, and men who belittle you, or, god forbid, are physically or emotionally abusive, are an absolute "No-No." Don't go there.

And if you are already there, walk away.

Yes, you can!

You deserve better than that.

Sometimes women end up in affairs with men they would never usually choose as a partner. They may be of a very different social sector, a different nationality or culture, or in some ways actually "no go areas" for them in their usual life such as men with a criminal record or an involvement with crime or drugs or alcohol.

Affairs of this sort are usually born out of a sense of boredom in an otherwise particularly ordered and structured life. A way to escape the mundane but comfortable existence they would never really truly want to give up but at the same time feel trapped in. Affairs with "totally unsuitable" men are usually entered into by married women who potentially have a lot to lose should the affair be discovered

If you are involved or on the verge of getting

involved with such a man please be very very careful. Walk away if you can. It is unlikely to work out in the long run, and no amount of excitement is worth getting involved in a world of crime or drugs, even if only on the edges.

Very often women who get involved with the kind of married man they would usually not even remotely consider are themselves married. More often than not they have a good life, but are bored and "miss something" in their life.

The case of Germany's richest woman was all over the media recently after she got involved with a criminal. He conned her out of literally millions, and when she refused to give him even more he tried to blackmail her with secretly recorded videotapes of their sexual encounters. Luckily she woke up and had the enormous strength to go to the police, at great cost to her family and reputation.

The lesson of this story is: Be very careful who you get involved with, as love makes us blind and we should not endanger our whole existence as well as our heart when we have an affair with a married man!

- 10 -
Not getting caught

It is actually possible to conduct an affair without directly causing hurt and wreaking havoc with the lives of those who are involuntarily affected (in other words: his wife and family.) If it messes up your life and/or his then that was your choice and by crossing "the line" you signed a contract that you do so at your own risk and accept that more likely than not you will get hurt. His wife and family did not enter into any such agreement so they must be protected at all cost.

This means you must not get caught.

It is a fascinating fact of life that women get found out far more rarely than men. Men tend to seriously underestimate the astuteness of women in general and their wives in particular, and lack the attention to detail women generally possess.

Men also have an unfortunate habit to impart details of their extra-marital excursions to their best mate after a pint or three. Best mate promptly tells his wife in a careless moment, she in turn tells her mate and before you can say "idle gossip kills" the whole thing is out in the open and it is only a matter of time before it arrives (probably suitably blown up out of all proportion) at the one set of ears it should never reach.

So our "perfect mistress" has the unenviable task of not only covering her own tracks intelligently and effectively, but also keeping an eagle eye on the man she is involved with.

At this point it is worth slipping in the little fact that out of the women who *do* get found out a shamefully large percentage cause the discovery either deliberately or recklessly. But we shall look at this particularly uunsavory way to conduct oneself elsewhere.

There are six main areas that need to be carefully watched to keep the affair where it belongs, namely between you and the man you are involved with.

- Alibis – i.e. where "she" believes him to be when he is with you
- Physical evidence – i.e. what not to leave on or around him
- Communication – i.e. how you communicate without leaving clues
- The paper trail – i.e. anything his wife might see on any 3rd party correspondence
- Witnesses – i.e. the danger of being seen at the wrong time in the wrong place by the wrong person
- Who to tell

The cardinal rule is to never, ever, under any circumstances underestimate his wife's sensitivity and intelligence. You may not want think of her as the smart, clever lady that she more than likely is (otherwise why would a man worthy of your affection have chosen to may her of all people in the first place?) but you will underestimate her at your peril.

So cover your tracks, watch yourself and him with eagle eyes, and do not get sloppy as the affair moves along.

Remember that this is your main responsibility in all of this, take whatever pride you can muster and fulfill this part of the bargain well. You will be able to look yourself into the eyes much more comfortably in the long run!

Alibis

By far the most fraught aspect of any affair is how he accounts for the time he spends with you. The main reason for this is that it is the one area that it almost invariably involves actual active lying (the other five main areas mainly involve avoiding leaving evidence in one form or the other). Traditionally, men are the worse liars of the sexes, and women possess the more sensitive antennae for anything that doesn't quite ring true. Women, with their inherently greater attention to detail and better memory for what was said by whom and when, also tend to notice discrepancies far more readily than a man in a similar situation would.

At a time when he has actually already forgotten that he even saw you on the 1st of March his wife may very well still be able to piece together where he said he was at that very date by a process of connecting things from her own life, such as the fact that it was Aunty Mary's birthday and she had to collect the kids on her way back from having those highlights (which were the wrong shade of blonde) put in at Mario's.

There isn't really an awful lot you can contribute here, his alibis are his job, but it won't hurt to keep an eye on how he goes about constructing them to protect him from the most obvious blunders. I know it's not the most romantic or passionate part of having an affair, but it is a necessary one unfortunately.

The more simply constructed an alibi is, the more likely it will hold. In the perfect affair alibis are largely unnecessary through a combination of personal and professional circumstances. If you are involved with a man who has always been away from home for varying lengths of time of their working day and week, especially when he has a wife with a similarly packed agenda you may find that the need for lengthy explanations regarding his whereabouts is minimal. Count yourself lucky.

Friends make dangerous allies when in need of an alibi. The most trusted friend will probably have to "help out" in an emergency, but generally it is advisable to keep the number of people who get dragged into your personal wicked web to the absolutely necessary minimum.

A very effective "friend" with whom he allegedly spends the time he is actually with you is one that does not exist. A non-existent friend will never inadvertently bump into your lover's wife in the supermarket while he is supposed to be playing golf with your man, or innocently call to speak to him while is supposed to be slaving over a presentation back at the office.

"Imaginary Friend" ("IF") also has the distinct

advantage of being entirely unable to fall out with your lover or causing trouble by spreading gossip.

"IF" has to be introduced carefully back at the happy home, slipped into an occasional conversation casually and frequently before he actually starts assuming his job as his alibi though.

Once his wife has got used to hearing about that particular person in connection with, say, work or the golf club, she will not get suspicious if said friend gradually grows into an integral part of your man's agenda.

"IF" should even be stored in your lover's mobile phone, his stored number being that of the "pay as you go" phone which you keep for emergencies, so if you have to call him for some reason at a risky time the number popping up on the display or in the call listing will not arouse any more suspicion than the odd carefully worded text message.

Of course "IF" also has an e-mail address.... It goes without saying that "IF" will NEVER leave a message on your lover's voice mail, mobile or, heaven forbid, at home, nor will "he" send text messages or e-mails with any clues as to the fact that he is more than a colleague / pal.

If at all possible your man should avoid providing alibis whenever possible. Have one readily prepared in case it is needed; yes, but only use it when directly questioned about his whereabouts. Surprisingly often this is the most effective solution, because a lie that was never uttered can never be uncovered.

Bad alibis are any that are all too easily found out (obviously). Friends that your lover and his wife have in common, especially when their own partners are also part of their social circle, usually make lousy alibis and should be avoided when possible.

Work usually provides good opportunities for alibis to be constructed, just make sure that he remembers what he said and when, and again try and explain to him that he should only use any story when it is necessary, and to try and avoid complicated stories he can't remember a week later.

Chances are his wife WILL remember and spot any inadvertent discrepancies, especially if her suspicions are aroused anyway.

Pay attention to the details of the stories he intends to tell. If his alibi is that he is playing rugby on a damp Sunday in November it simply won't do if he comes home freshly showered but with the rugby gear in his bag still clean and smelling of fabric softener.

Physical evidence – i.e. what not to leave on or around him

This is really largely your job. You must make sure that when the man you are involved with comes home, or his wife gets into his car / phone / correspondence / office there is no hint of a suggestion that you exist.

Whilst I generally stress that it is far healthier for the mistress's sanity to think about "the wife" as little as humanly possible this is one area where, at least in an abstract manner, doing so is unavoidable. Like it or not, she shares his house, she shares his bed more likely than not, she probably washes and irons or at least handles his clothes and she will probably open or at least see his bills and statements.

As a woman she will be quite sensitive to clues, and possess an attention to detail that most probably exceeds his. So it is your responsibility to make sure that there is nothing that could cause her to stop and think about, nothing that hints at anything being unusual, and nothing that could be explained by him having an affair.

Physical marks

NEVER! No love bites (if you are past the age of consent they are a bit childish anyway, be serious!) and no scratched backs. If you can not guarantee that you have complete control over your fingernails at all times then cut them to a safe length or develop the unfortunate habit of biting them - you'll have reason enough to do the latter while waiting by the phone at some point or the other anyway.

Make-Up and Perfume (yours)

Repeat after me: "There is no such thing as Make-Up that will not leave marks on a white shirt." Whatever the glossy ads try to make us believe, we have all spent too much time trying to remove a smudge from an own favorite item to believe it.

So either go extremely easy on the offending

products, or make sure his clothes do not come into close contact with them. Waterproof mascara helps a great deal, so does taking off his white shirt before getting close and personal.

Crying on his chest / shoulder is not only bad form for any self respecting mistress, it's also a sure-fire way to leave marks that can be not only spotted, but also identified correctly by almost any wife.

Perfume as well as scented lotions and potions are another area that requires close attention. Obviously you want him to smell them on you, but you sure as hell don't want HER to smell them on him.

So don't smother yourself in your favorite scent, even if it IS the impossibly expensive latest "must have" he bought you for your birthday.... If possible, put on your scent a couple of hours before you are due to meet, and don't liberally splash it all over yourself directly but spray it in the air and walk through the mist. That will suffice, and not leave him reeking of "Eau de Evidence" when he gets home.

If he showers before he goes home (good idea always, out of a sense of decency as well as to avoid detection) make sure he uses the same products he uses at home or get a set of unscented products such as those produced for people with allergies and sensitive skin. He needs to arrive home looking and smelling as if he was where he was supposed to be.

Scents, clothes and gifts (his)

Chances are you will occasionally buy him something, be it a particular aftershave or that set of British racing green silk boxer shorts he so liked in your favorite store. That's fine of course, but they should stay away from his home.

Women are usually quite sensitive to sudden changes in a man's behavior and habits. If his wife has been married to a man that wears the 3-pack cotton briefs his mom buys him every Christmas she will definitely view those silk boxer shorts with more than a smidgeon of suspicion.

The same goes for the sudden appearance of a bottle of "Egoiste" aftershave on his shelf in the bathroom cabinet. Not too many men buy these things for themselves as a matter of course, so either keep these clues at your place or make sure they won't arouse suspicion if they do make their way into "her" territory. (Don't cringe please, it *is* just that, like it or not.)

In fact any little or larger present you buy for him needs to pass the "If I was someone's wife, would seeing this make me go *Hmmmm???*" test. If the answer is "yes" then the present should stay away from his wife's field of vision at all times.

Leaving clues in his car, his home or pockets

If you ever meet at the home he shares with his wife (dangerous and borderline bad manners in my humble opinion but not always avoidable) then you absolutely MUST make sure that you are painstakingly aware of every single item of clothing, every accessory, every bit of jewelry, every receipt and other item you could inadvertently walk out without.

In such a situation "less is more." The less little potential unexploded bombs you enter their house with the less likely you are to leave one behind to explode at some point in the near or more distant future when your left stocking chokes the vacuum cleaner.

Exercise the same care and attention about anything you do in his car too. If you smoke you must not use the car's ashtray unless you smoke the same brand he does and are not wearing any lipstick. Keep your handbag firmly shut in case of a small item falling out and hiding under the passenger seat until detected.

Make sure he does not have anything in his pockets before he goes home that will betray you. His wife may not be the type to search through his things with a suspicious mind, but she may be quite innocently checking his jeans before sticking them into the washing machine and there are many little items that could cause quite unnecessary hassle so it pays to make sure the situation does not arise in the first place.

Communicating without arousing suspicion

One of the unfortunate side-effects of having an affair is that one can't just pick up the phone to call the object of one's desire whenever one feels like it. But of course you knew that before you started having an affair with him (yes you did, you may just not have been aware of the implications). So let's look at ways of being able to communicate without risking detection.

In general it is a good idea to keep any electronic and telephone communication to a minimum at all times when his wife could observe any of it.

Notes and letters should, if at all possible, be avoided because they can be found and read. Cards and little love-letters must not enter the marital home at any time; marriages have imploded years after an affair had already ended just because one or the other partner opened a long forgotten envelope carelessly tucked away in an old magazine in the attic!

Here we can use our trusted "IF" very effectively though. He can send a text message to your lover's mobile phone or an e-mail requesting contact without arousing suspicion should the message be inadvertently been seen by the wrong eyes. Our "IF" was called Malcolm McKenzie by the way, don't ask why – it seemed a good idea at the time....

If you are the kind of "couple" that like to whisper sweet nothings into each other's ears when not together it complicates matters. Under no circumstances should you call him on, or let him call you from, his landline at home or a cell phone if his wife has access to the invoice. In these days of itemized billing even our dear Imaginary Friend will start to wear thin as an excuse if the invoices indicate a pattern of lengthy conversations late at night.

However, cell phones are cheap enough and can be fed with "pay as you go" prepaid cards, removing the threat of any physical evidence of the "itemized bill" kind. Caution should still be exercised even with these, train your lover to empty out his call-lists (both made and received) as a matter of course, and to delete any text messages (sent and received) immediately just in case the phone falls into the wrong hands.

Under no circumstances that I can readily think of should you ever call him at home. It is simply not worth it, even from a withheld or blocked number. Calling and hanging up when his wife answers is incredibly bad manners and will serve no purpose than arousing her suspicion and quite probably (and rightly) his anger.

If he calls you from his landline (which again he should not do if at all possible) he should get into the habit of dialing the number of his own mobile phone after speaking to you. This will mean the old "last number re-dial" trick will not work should his wife for some more or less innocent reason try it, and is easily explained by saying he could not find his mobile phone hence called the number to locate it by sound.

If they have the type of fancy set-up which lists the last 10 or whatever numbers at a push of a button then any calls from that phone to your number are out of bounds completely.

Unless he has a secretary that plays bridge with his wife phoning him at work can be a much safer way to talk, but again a degree of discretion is advisable.

E-mail is only ever safe if his wife will not have access to his e-mail account. Use his work e-mail address if he has one AND if his work e-mails are safe from prying eyes at home.

You may not think his wife to be computer-savvy enough to find shreds of evidence on the computer at home, but you would be surprised and possibly horrified what can be hidden in the history of a browser, so the utmost caution must be exercised if using this form of communication where his wife could conceivably have access to it.

There are now gadgets such as key loggers and Bluetooth devices which allow every typed word, every call, every text message and every e-mail to be reconstructed at the push of a button. His wife may not be totally proficient with computers and technical devices but if her suspicions are aroused you can be sure that she could find out how to use those things if she really wanted to!

For absolute emergencies you should have agreed a code between the two of you which tells him to get in touch with you as soon as possible. Keep this for real emergencies only though, not just because you want to hear his voice or to give him an earful because he has not called you when he promised.

For this you need a trusted MALE friend who can call the marital home (preferably withholding his number) and then pass on a seemingly innocuous message. Very devious couples may have a set of "codes" agreed, each with it's own real meaning, but for most situations one fake message is enough to remember and the patience and good will of the male friend who has to make the call should not be abused by making a habit out of it either.

The paper trail – i.e. anything his wife might see on any 3rd party correspondence

Just as you need to avoid his wife finding an unusual number cropping up at unusual times on the phone bill, you should make sure that no unusual items appear on his credit card bill! Not only do any exceptional items of spending arouse a wife's suspicion in more ways than one (there is the aspect of her wondering why money is being spent at all without her knowledge, not just on whom it is being spent).

So evenings out should be paid for in cash or using your own card (this is the 21st century, you ARE allowed to pay your way) if his wife has access to the credit card account. There are also prepaid credit cards which can be applied for online and provide online statements. Larger expenditures (which should be avoided anyway as it is not fair for you to not only sleep with her husband but to deplete the household finances as well) such as expensive tickets for a play or a weekend away can be booked using this prepaid credit card without leaving any trace.

When doing, booking or buying anything which could in any way cause any correspondence to be sent you should use your address and not his. I'm quite sure you agree that no wife deserves to find a letter stating "Dear Mr. and Mrs._____, We hope you enjoyed your recent stay at the Most Excellent Hotel, Brighton, and would like to entice you back by offering you a special discount for the honeymoon suite on your next visit."

By using your address rather than that of the marital home you can quite effectively skirt around issues like these. And issues are always much better avoided than dealt with once the shit has already hit the fan.

Other items to watch out for are restaurant or hotel receipts (need to be disposed of or hidden at his office/place of work), gas card bills or receipts if they do not support his alibis – he can not have put fuel into his car in Bath when he was supposed to be playing cricket in Cheltenham that very day. Do not rely on his wife to not make the connection, she may not but if she does there'll be hell to pay. Basically anything that contains a date or a place or both needs to be kept out of her reach. Better safe than sorry!

Witnesses – the danger of being seen at the wrong time in the wrong place by the wrong person

This is a hard one. Basically the more you get out and about together the more likely it becomes that you may be spotted by someone you'll wish had not seen you.

In an ideal world you and the illegitimate object of your desire live in different towns, have a different circle of friends and don't work at the same place.

However, this is probably not the most likely scenario as you must have met somewhere, somehow in the first place.

Going out together, be it to a restaurant or a pub, a trip to the theatre or cinema, will be a rare pleasure unless you do so at a town far enough away to minimize bumping into people who could wonder what he is doing there and who you are. They may not immediately blow the whistle on you, but few things ruin a much longed for and carefully planned special evening out as effectively as suddenly coming face to face with his next door neighbor over a cozy meal.

The problem with NOT going out (i.e. staying at your place *all* the time) is of course the feeling of the whole "relationship" being based on just sex.

Even if that were the case it is not something you want to be reminded of, so getting out and about doing relatively "normal" couple things is important for your own sanity if nothing else.

To minimize the danger of being seen by the wrong eyes at the wrong time you should not only pick places which are a safe distance from his home and avoid places where his wife's usual circle of friends could easily come walking round the corner, you should also make sure that you choose restaurant tables that are not visible to passers by, and go into the cinema or theatre as late as possible to avoid being sitting targets for prying eyes in the line.

Weekends away somewhere totally different from time to time are perfect to make up for a lack of going out normally, and if you are lucky he has a job that requires at least some degree of business travel, that way not only might you be able to accompany him, any trips which are of a completely NON-business nature can fairly easily be disguised as such without arousing suspicion.

Remember to book in under your name if there is any chance of his wife questioning a hotel booking, just to be on the safe side.

Obviously you will make sure that his bags contain only HIS things before checking out, and that there is no evidence on anything he takes back to the marital home that could hint at the true nature of his trip. If he was supposed to be at a sales conference in Newcastle, a piece of heart-shaped Brighton Rock, or a couple of shells carelessly picked up during a romantic evening stroll on the beach and promptly forgotten in a jacket pocket, will not require a mastermind to interpret quite correctly.

Who to tell

When we are in the middle of something really exciting, something that touches many aspects of our lives, something that causes exhilaration and pain in equal measure, we tend to want to share it with our nearest and dearest.

Sometimes we just have to talk about what affects us deeply, have a good moan about the impossible way "he" behaved, or simply cry on a good friend's shoulder.

You may find many of your female friends to be somewhat less than thrilled to lend a sympathetic ear to your tales of woe or accounts of your last exciting encounter, and frankly it's dangerous as well.

The less people know about it the less likely is one of them to cause the discovery of your affair. If you absolutely must confide in someone you would be wise to choose a person who does not know him personally (and for God's sake, never ever as much as DREAM of telling anyone who knows his wife!).

A sympathetic best friend is worth her weight in gold, but don't abuse her willingness to support you in something she may not find particularly laudable herself. For obvious reasons that "sympathetic best friend" is more likely to be found amongst your single or divorced circle of female friends, and not amongst those who are themselves more or less happily married.

Oh, as an (to me at least) amusing side-note: Watch how those who know about you having an affair start keeping a beady eye on you whenever you come within approximately 10 yards of their own men. Another reason to keep one's mouth shut whenever possible.

-11-
Do No Harm

I have had endless discussions, even arguments about this (for me) very important cardinal rule. The majority of my friends seem to be adamant that by the very act of getting involved with a man who is married or attached to another woman one is breaking it.

Be that as it may, this chapter is about understanding that we must not inflict any additional harm onto anyone involved, especially and most importantly those who could be affected without having any choice in the matter.

We may feel an overwhelming urge to kid ourselves into thinking that we quite accidentally ended up in the situation we find ourselves in, but that's nonsense.

Every Other Woman in every married man's life did, at some point, make a conscious decision to sleep with a man she shouldn't. Her lover made a conscious decision to stray. Frankly provided neither of you was under the influence of hallucinogenic drugs at the time there was a choice made to do what is being done.

But I need not labor that point, we looked at the matter of excuses and explanations already so let's move swiftly on.

His wife and his children, if they have any, made no

such choice. So to inflict pain on them deliberately, recklessly or carelessly in any way shape or form is not acceptable.

This, by definition, means that the perfect Other Woman will do everything within her power to prevent him being found out (this one is also in her own interest as nothing ends more affairs and ends them both rapidly and comprehensively as the wife getting wind of it - whatever he may whisper into your ears between the sheets).

It also means that you accept that the main part of his spare time will be spent with them, not you. It means accepting that his money will be spent on them, not on you or on doing things with you.

It means living with the fact that not seeing him when he is on holiday and at birthdays, Christmas, family days of any kind really, is how it is, and how it should be.

Having suffered a long three weeks in August while the object of my desire was sunning himself on some Italian beach with his family, and then staying carefully away from images of them all under the tree at Christmas, I certainly know how hard this can all be.

Make sure you have a wonderful set of understanding friends, as there are days when you will most definitely need them.

You should make a deal with yourself (and inform your lover accordingly) that whilst you are having an affair and want to keep having that affair you will not act in any way that will bring harm and heartbreak to those who are wronged by your decision and actions.

You hope that one day he will leave his wife to be with you? Well, this is something every Other Woman probably considers at least in a purely hypothetical way, even if it is not her deep and overwhelming wish or aim. He may even mention the possibility as a more or less likely future development but you should neither count on it, believe in it (to avoid the bitter disappointment that will follow more likely than not) or live your life waiting for that day to come.

Most cheating men never leave their wives for their Other Woman and if that is your declared aim or the only reason why you are staying in this affair then the statistics say you have no business having an affair in the first place.

What you must never ever do is actively try to make him leave his wife. Quite apart from the fact that he is having an affair with you because it's more fun and less hassle than being at home (and that making his time with you less fun and more hassle is MOST unlikely to make him want to swap hasslesome place 1 with hasslesome place 2...) it is not your job to put pressure on him in any way shape or form.

And never ever even think about forcing the issue by either risking his wife finding out, or committing the ultimate "Other Woman Crime" by actually telling her.

The pain you would cause by doing so is something that nothing in this world is worth, not even that man. Probably *especially* not that man.

So depending on how you feel about the whole subject matter *please*: "Do no harm" or "Do no more harm than you are inflicting anyway by doing what you are doing already."

"What about the harm it is all doing to *me*?????" I hear you ask. Well, frankly, that's just tough luck.

First of all it is doing as much harm to you as you are choosing to let it. And secondly you presumably entered into that potentially harmful situation with your eyes wide open and at least a portion of your brain in working order.

If you cough because you're a smoker don't complain about it.

If you play with fire chances are you'll get burnt.

Have an affair and you could quite possibly get hurt. It's hardly rocket science, is it?

Just remember that all this was our *choice*. And we have the choice to walk away from it at any time (Oh YES you could). Those who had no choice in the matter (in other words his wife and family) deserve to be protected from what we are doing.

-12-
Looking at the bright side

We all know that being involved with a married man has some serious disadvantages. There is absolutely no point in listing them, or dwelling on them because none of them will really come as a surprise to you.

Let us instead look at the bright side for a change, the advantages of being "The Other Woman" rather than "the wife."

We play this little game of "Count your Blessings" because there are many of having an affair with a wonderful man (if he wasn't a wonderful man surely we would not be having an affair with him in the first place now, would we!?) which beat having him around us all the time.

How many long term married women think back wistfully to those heady days when their love was young and fresh and exciting, when everyday life had not yet taken over? How many wish back the excitement of waiting for him to call, getting ready to go on a date, trying on 3 different outfits to make sure they're looking their best, racing around the house with butterflies in their stomachs checking if everything is in the right place and the candles within reach to be lit much later?

Almost invariably this giddy excitement wanes in the face of life, work, mortgage, the school run, the cooking, and all the rest that clutters up our lives.

But when we are the Other Woman chances are we still experience most or even all of that (in between the bad bits) Some of the "best affairs" are almost stuck in a perpetual time warp which closely resembles the early days of dating someone in a really good way.

What is rare and difficult to attain is always all the more desirable for it. Snatched moments can be sweeter than whole weeks, a stolen kiss more passionate and spiced up further by danger, promise and regret. Not for us the perfunctory peck on the cheek that's become the routine in many long term relationships.

Sex (we will, at this point, simply assume you do have sex with him) again can be exceptional if you manage not to let guilt or anger ruin the fun for you (if you do - *bad* move, why bother if you don't enjoy it!?).

Never underestimate what a powerful aphrodisiac adrenaline is, nor how even the "nicest" woman can be turned on by that heady mixture of desire and guilt.

The excitement of never knowing for sure how things will turn out does grate on one's nerves at times (more or less depending on your individual nature) but it also undoubtedly adds to the attraction.

Chances are *he* will be at his best behavior too when he sees you! He might be a couch potato and a bit of a bore at home if he has long since run out of exciting topics of conversation with his wife (or she's heard them all and won't listen anymore) - but he will be at his sparkling best when he is with you.

Men have affairs because something is missing in their lives (incidentally this is something wives would do well to remember), and often they miss that "something" within and about *themselves* as much as in their marriage.

They miss the smart, funny, cute guy they think they once were, they miss the intelligent conversations they remember (rightly or wrongly) being able to impress the ladies with, they miss the adoration in a woman's eyes when they've done something adorable or the happy laughter they used to be able to magic on her face when saying something particularly witty.

So when a man starts an affair he tries harder than he has tried at home for years. Chances are you're getting the best of him, and seeing a side his wife hasn't seen in quite a while, if ever.

And he'll keep on trying provided you keep things alive between the two of you. When either or both quit trying to make it special it's time to call it quits altogether.

The absence of the disadvantages is as much of an advantage as all of the above.

You don't (I hope) have to tidy up after him, someone else picks up his socks from the bathroom floor, washes his clothes, irons his shirts, handles the shopping, supervises the cleaner, books his car in for a service, prepares the Sunday roast, buys the Christmas presents for his extended family and remembers his secretary's birthday. (If you are doing more than a couple of the above regularly you are in danger of assuming the role of a second wife; with the disadvantages of a being a mistress and none of the advantages of being the wife - take a long hard look at the situation and change it.... It's a bad deal!)

Contrary to popular belief the average mistress is not a sad moppet who sits at home waiting for the phone to ring as a sign that the man she is involved with may have found a gap in his busy schedule and wants to see her.

She is a smart woman with a life of her own, quite possibly a demanding job, a good social life that does not involve him, friends to see, places to go, hobbies.

Basically she has a life!

If that does not sound like you, or, even worse, if this sounds like you before you met him, pull the emergency brake immediately and either *get "a life"* back, or build yourself one up.

It is absolutely not acceptable for any woman to sit around wasting her life (or even just her precious free evenings) waiting for any man to fit her into whatever other commitments he has.

Being lonely and needy is also not particularly attractive - so bear that in mind. It's obviously perfectly understandable that you might generally want to see a bit more of him than you can due to the circumstances, but frankly that is part of the course and part of the excitement, and most men will either get bored with, or irritated by (or both if she's unlucky), a mistress that is just moping about unless she can see him.

It also puts them under a subtle (or not so subtle) type of pressure and if he is only borderline sensitive then he will feel it. We all know how men react to pressure, especially emotional pressure so we may be shooting ourselves an own goal.

So looking at it that way the mistress is really getting a pretty good deal, she can have her cake and eat it too if she plays things right, she can lead a near "single-girl type" of life with most of the advantages, and she still has him (albeit on a more or less frequent part time basis) with all the advantages of being in a "relationship" of sorts.

Is it all going to end in tears? Well yes, as it happens, it probably will. And those tears are just as likely to be mainly ours. But if that's the price we know we are going to have to pay (we DO know that, really, deep down, don't we!?) then we sure as hell should be making the most of it while it lasts, enjoy it as much as we can, and make memories worth treasuring for ever.

Live life and your affair to the fullest, and in such away that you can look back one day and say

"Je Ne Regrette Rien"

-13-
Having "A Happy Affair"

When I first started to speak to Other Women in the course of researching this book I rather naively assumed that most of them were really quite happy with the relationship they had. Obviously there are numerous downsides to having an affair as opposed to what conventional wisdom calls a "real relationship" but I did not expect a lot of women to be fundamentally unhappily involved with a married man.

So it came as a considerable surprise to me to find that quite a few of the women I spoke to were actually really quite unhappy. They were unhappy because they were in a relationship with a man they loved with all their heart, but who was married to someone else.

I tried to understand why they stay in a situation that breaks their heart over and over again, but I have to confess that I haven't yet quite managed to get to the bottom of it.

So rather than dwelling on their unhappiness at being in a situation of their own choosing, let us try and see what the difference between the happy and the unhappy Other Woman is, and how the unhappy Other Woman could change her attitude to the affair in order to be less unhappy about the way things are going.

We may not always be able to change a situation, but we can usually at least control our attitude to it.

The main source of unhappiness is certainly the fact that the man we are involved with is married. But frankly that particular bit of information does not come as news to us, now does it?

The problem with wanting him to not be married is that the more we dwell on the fact that he is, and the more we try to get him to change the fact, the less likely he becomes to do so.

We all know the statistics which predict that only a diminishingly small number of men will ever leave their wives to be with their mistress. This bit is not exactly news to us, but what may come as a surprise is that the majority of the Other Women I met and spoke to who *did* end up with their married lover had neither expected it nor ever asked him to leave his wife.

They were reasonably happy in their affairs, they gave it all they could like we do in any relationship that is important to us (at least in the beginning) and they were eventually, often to their own considerable surprise, rewarded with him leaving his wife entirely off his own back and under his own steam.

So whilst I would not really want to suggest that "having a happy affair" is a good tactic to get your married lover to leave his wife for you, there certainly seems to be a real correlation between those happy affairs and those who ended up as "more than an affair" in due course.

And as if to prove the point – the women who told

me about how unhappy they were in their affair because they so desperately wanted their married lovers to leave their wives were the ones that didn't end up with him in the end. The affairs ended because everyone was simply becoming too unhappy for it being worth the risk and the hassle.

So how can an Other Woman make sure she is having a "Happy Affair?"

It's fairly simple, really. We just have to accept that what we are having, at least for the time being and probably the foreseeable future, is an affair. We have to swallow the fact that we currently have the choice of being happily involved with a married man, or being unhappily involved with a married man, and then act on that choice.

I personally am not prepared to waste my precious time and my equally precious emotions on an unhappy relationship or in a waiting-loop of any description. It seems a pretty pointless exercise, if one wants to be brutally honest for a moment.

Once we have managed to let go of the notion that the here and now is in some way not the real thing, but a stepping stone, or a prison sentence to be endured until such a time when the status quo changes, we can actually enjoy the affair for all the reasons we chose to begin it in the first place.

If I may use my own story as an example: If I had spoilt what was a most wonderful affair with an absolutely wonderful man by being unhappy about the restrictions the situation applied to it I would be heartbroken now. The man I was involved with died before we could attempt "stage 2" of our relationship, and all I have left is the memories.

But – honestly, "Oh what memories we made...."

They are completely unspoiled memories, never poisoned by any bickering, we never once argued, and when we were together it was absolute joy. Yes, I missed him when I didn't see him, but basically I was rarely "unhappy" about the affair, with the obvious exception of the horrible weeks between his wife finding out and the two of them splitting up when we were in a "No Contact" type of situation.

The reason I am bringing this story up is because it actually demonstrates why we should try making our affair as happy as we possibly can. Because that may be all it might ever be. There may well never be a "Happy Ever After" for the married men we are involved in and ourselves. That should, however, not ruin the present. In other words the affair should really be seen as a reason to be happy rather than as something to be endured until real happiness can catch up with us.

If we can see the relationship we have with these men as something to be happy about as it is (at least for the time being) we can avoid becoming an "unhappy Other Woman" who suffers an unhappy situation entirely of her own making.

Relationships of any kind are to be enjoyed first and foremost for what they are, and only secondly (if at all) for what they may or may not become one day. This concept is hard to grasp for some, who appear to be in the affair purely because of the desperate hope that one day he will leave his wife. But frankly if we allow ourselves to conduct our affair in that way we will be unhappy. And an unhappy relationship is one that isn't really worth having in the vast majority or cases.

Interestingly the majority of the Other Women who *do* eventually end up making the transition from Other Woman to *Only* Woman tend to be the ones who were in what I would class as "Happy Affairs."

Having a "Happy Affair" could therefore help to achieve the very status that those who are so unhappy about being in an affair are craving. In fact in many cases it could be argued that these unhappy Other Women are effectively preventing what they want, by ruining what they do have in the desperate quest of turning it into something else.

If you want to avoid wasting months or even years of your precious life on an unhappy relationship then you should exercise your right to choose: Just as you have chosen to be in this affair you actually do have the choice to end it.

Or you could choose to make the most of what you and your married man have now, to enjoy it while it lasts, and to make each other happy.

Anything else, any transition of the relationship into something quite different, is another matter altogether which can be addressed if and when it happens. And believe me, such a transition is more likely to occur if you don't spoil the present by being an unhappy woman who lives only for an uncertain future that may or may not ever happen.

The best foundation for a happy future with your married man is, in other words, a happy affair in the present!

- 14 -
The Waiting Game

One of the most irritating and thoroughly demoralizing aspects to life as the Other Woman is the fact that so much time, and really so much of "life" is spent waiting.

Waiting for him to call, waiting for him to come and visit, waiting for him to find an hour here, an afternoon there, an evening, a night or even a weekend if the gods are smiling, and last but by no means least – waiting for something in the relationship to change. Waiting for him to leave his wife, maybe when the kids are older, the mortgage paid off, the career more established, or any number of things which appear to be, currently, obstacles in the way of what the Other Woman sees as her chance of true happiness with her married man at last.

Waiting is generally a gigantic waste of time, unless it is filled with useful or entertaining pastimes. When I hear about women who spend hours and days staring at a phone desperately willing it to ring I could literally scream.

Yes, the temptation is there of course, and "Other Women" – especially at the beginning of an affair – are tempted to rearrange their schedule to suit his, and keep big chunks of spare time free just to be available at the drop of a hat in case he calls and wants to see her.

Not only is that a waste of time, it is also a dangerous way to behave, it is all too easy to neglect friendships or even lose them because of too many cancelled get-togethers with no real explanation. You are not likely to say "Sorry, can't make dinner as planned because I am sleeping with a married man tonight instead," to all but the very closest friends, or at least not if you are wise enough to keep the number of people who know about your affair down to a sensible minimum.

To stand a chance of a happy affair the Other Woman must adopt a realistic attitude to balance waiting for him to be in touch and carrying on with her life. The best attitude to adopt is really to carry on as if he did not exist most of the time, making a concerted effort to spend adequate time with old friends, making an effort to meet some new people, not to let hobbies and sport slide and pushing ahead with the career if that has been getting a little less attention than it deserves due to that married man in her life.

Not only will this considerably ease the irritation of waiting, it will make for a much happier, much more contented, much less impatient and irritated partner for him when he DOES get to see her.

And it has never hurt to not be *too* available; it is not healthy for a man's ego or his attitude towards his Other Woman to know that she will simply drop everything at every possible and impossible time to get to spend a few hours with him. It will not exactly breed respect, nor will it make him want to be a little bit clearer and thoughtful regarding the way their meetings are planned and scheduled.

That was the one aspect of "waiting," the aspect that affects us from one day to the next, a week at a time or a month maybe. The other aspect is the way we wait for life as we know it to change because we live in the hope that one day we will be "more" than "just" the Other Woman, that one day we will have him to ourselves, and have a "proper" relationship with him, live with him.

In other words the Other Woman spends days, weeks, months, years, sometimes even decades, waiting for him to leave his wife.

As far as happiness goes, the happiest Other Women are those who have either given up waiting or have never done too much waiting around in the first place.

When I was researching this book I spoke to a lot of wonderful women who, between them, have spent centuries in affairs with married men. A surprising number had been seeing their married lover for over 5 years, over 10 years, and even much longer than that. That was one of the most surprising aspects because at the time I had not even considered that women would spend *that* long in the shadows, *that* long living a lie, *that* long having to be careful what they say, do and where they say and do it — and still hang around.

Obviously many of those in very long relationships with married men have seen a lot of "We will be together once ..." dates come and go and the men still remain securely married, and the Other Woman still hangs on. Those women have, for the most part, accepted that he will never leave his wife, and eventually mostly no longer particularly want him to. I guess there comes a point where you arrange yourself with all kinds of circumstances, and after a number of years they have seen the benefits in the setup as it is, and either don't, or no longer wish to rock the boat by changing the status quo that dramatically.

The other set of stories, which I have to admit scared and touched me equally, were those of women who spent years waiting, years being the ever supportive Other Woman in the background, and patiently (or as patiently as they could manage) hung on while the kids grew up, the mortgage was paid off, the career reached its pinnacle. They did so just to finally then see him leave his wife *at last* – and them as well, either to strike out alone as a single man or straight into the arms of a new woman.

I remember very clearly watching the funeral of Francois Mitterand, one time President of France.

His funeral was attended by his wife and their children (obviously) and also by his long term mistress with their daughter. At the time the last thing that was on my mind at the time was affairs with married men but I recall very clearly how two aspects of that scene struck me: First, the dignity and class with which these two women dealt with what could not have been a very easy situation, and secondly how his mistress must have felt. I wondered if she had spent the many years she was Francois Mitterand's Other Woman waiting for their relationship to change, to now stand at the grave of the man she loved for a long long time.

If she did it must have hurt twice as badly, knowing that the wait was finally over and that he had never taken that step.

The fact is that few married men leave their wives, and the longer the affair goes on the less likely they are to actually do so. It is also a fact that of the small percentage that do leave their wife and family, many go back (oh how heartbreaking *that* must be – worse even than if he had never made that step at all) and then there are those who leave their wife and break up with their Other Woman at or around the same time.

Yes, there are women who wait, and whose wait is rewarded when they finally, after months or years end up with the man they were having the affair with, but it is not the norm. It is not something the Other Woman should base her life on, and if it happens it would be best to come as a pleasant surprise (how pleasant it remains for how long is a whole other can of worms dealt with elsewhere).

But statistically these are in the minority. The reason why people keep saying, "But I know many couples where the man left the wife and is now living with or married to his former mistress," is because they don't even know about the many affairs that have been and still are going on secretly around them, where women have waited in vain, and men have not ever left their wives.

Waiting is something that comes with the territory I'm afraid, and I won't pretend otherwise. Waiting is one of the hardest aspects of having an affair with a married man, and one of the most damaging. So it is something we should deal with carefully, deal with sensibly and realistically, and keep to the absolute minimum we have to cope with.

Doing so is not only going to keep us (relatively) sane, it will also be making our life much fuller and more rewarding.

The worst thing any Other Woman can experience is that she may have wasted so much time and so much of her life waiting, not enjoying life to the full, and at some point has to look back on all that wasted time with regret.

Whilst the irritation of waiting can not really be avoided altogether it *is* possible to have an affair with a married man and not waste too much time waiting, by making him and the relationship with him apart of our life, not the be all and end all and center of our universe.

If we make sure our life is full of other aspects, useful aspects such as furthering our career, joyful aspects such as a great set of close friends to share our life and time with, and interesting aspects like hobbies, maybe sports and culture, we help ourselves not to become victims!

Regret is not something we should encourage and create. We should be working on carrying on with our life and making happy memories with the men we are involved with. One day, those memories may well be all we are left with – and too much wasted time, and certainly too much wasted life, would be too high a price to pay.

Basically that means that whilst we are all afflicted by the waiting game to some degree, waiting will be as significant as we allow it to be. We *can* actually fill the time we spend waiting with useful, joyful, entertaining endeavors. We can wait for a phone call while spending a fun evening out with friends. We can wait for him to leave his wife while getting on with our life as if we weren't waiting.

Once again we actually have control over just how much we let this affect us, practically and emotionally. We "just" need to learn how to exercise that control. That, of course, is the hard bit, but we should, for our own sake, take control of the waiting we do just as we take control of the other aspects of having an affair as far as the way we deal with it ourselves is concerned.

- 15 -

Matters of conscience and guilt

Nothing spoils anything we could ever possibly think of doing as effectively as being constantly dragged down by our own conscience and feelings of guilt.

Obviously it would be quite unrealistic to expect those who are conducting affairs with married men to be completely free of occasional, or even frequent stirrings of a guilty conscience about what they do.

But this should not be allowed to take over or ruin the relationship. Once we have entered into the affair with both eyes wide open we have accepted that we are doing something that isn't right and at the same time has the potential to hurt those who have not chosen the situation. His wife and family, in other words.

Frankly no amount of guilty feelings will actually make the facts of the matter any "better," so those of us who can keep them to a minimum are really just doing everyone involved a favor. There is no point wallowing in puddles of guilt, unless we intend to change what we feel guilty about doing. In fact I must confess that I have always viewed overly dramatic accounts of how an Other Woman is constantly wrecked by her own feelings of guilt with a degree of suspicion.

It is one thing to feel guilty about having done something that turned out to be harmful to others with hindsight, but to indulge (if I may call it that) in too much of it while still carrying on doing the very thing one is feeling so guilty about sometimes smacks of hypocrisy .

I am not a fan of making excuses, but when we are the single Other Woman in the life of a married man we would be well advised to limit the degree of guilt we allow ourselves to wallow in.

Put bluntly, we are not the ones who are cheating on our wife, and as long as we take all reasonable precautions to avoid her finding out about us we are not directly responsible for any misery she may experience. The wife in our particular triangle is the responsibility of her husband and whilst a degree of conscience is natural, and probably healthy, there is no real point in letting it ruin what we are evidently not willing to end anyway.

Those Other Women who are very religious tend to have the hardest time with those feelings of guilt and conscience, because almost every religion views affairs with married men as something that is to be condemned.

There is no patent recipe that allows us to get rid of those feelings, but we should accept them for what they are in the context of our affairs. Feelings that should be acknowledged and then tightly controlled, unless we are fully prepared to act on them immediately by ending the affair.

Some Other Women have managed to come to some kind of truce with their own values to a degree that they can conduct their affair with the minimum of interference by guilt. They try to do as little harm as possible under the circumstances, and squelch any undue amounts of guilty feelings in the bud.

Others, such as a very good friend of mine, adopt the attitude that once we knowingly enter an affair with a married man we allow our conscience to be effectively amputated as far as the affair is concerned. Said very good friend actually compared the occasional stirrings of a guilty conscience she experiences with the phantom pains amputees feel. Memories of where there once was a conscience rather than the conscience itself.

The fact remains that unless we are prepared to stop what we are feeling guilty about we might as well stop feeling an undue degree of guilt about it. All it does is ruin what the relationship we have chosen to be in, without doing anyone any good at all.

-16-
Sex

We will keep this short as there are more than enough books on how to have sex and enjoy it, and will simply assume that you know what you are doing in this department.

Nor is it particularly useful to try and compose a list of places to meet and get close and personal in – I will leave that to you and your man's imagination.

There are, however, various aspects to having a sexual relationship with a man who is married or attached to someone else that differ significantly to those that pop up within a conventional relationship.

Never underestimate what a powerful aphrodisiac adrenaline is. Or how a bit of danger and guilt can spice up what might be, under more conventional circumstances, a pretty mundane and average encounter of the physical kind.

It is easy to let oneself fall victim of the illusion that sex with "him" is the best thing since sliced bread, and so unique and mind-blowing that we can't possibly do without.

Essentially no one can tell you what to feel or how to handle your sexual encounters, but be very careful to see the tricks that your hormones play on your senses as just what they are.

Enjoy it, have fun, make each other happy, by all means! Don't let those feelings deceive you into turning the whole subject matter into something it is not though!

Another aspect worth thinking about is how to deal with "not feeling like it today." People who have affairs tend to, by definition, be unable to spend as much time with each other as one or even both would like. This makes that little time more special and valuable (or at least it should) and women especially are reluctant to ruin those "special" hours if they can avoid it.

But there are multiple reasons why a mistress may not be feeling compelled to tear "his" clothes off before he is even fully through the door every time she sees him. One of the most common reasons for a sudden lack of sexual "frisson" can be a conscious or subconscious desire to not be a pure sex object.

The idea that an affair is based purely or mainly on sex does not fit too comfortably into the picture a woman paints of herself and her relationships. So by not having sex she may be trying to convince herself that there is more to the whole affair than "it."

Men are, in general, less burdened by the fear of being a sex-object so may not understand that line of reasoning, especially if it is not explained to them. And because most mistresses worth their salt have long understood that rare stolen hours of being together are absolutely not the time for disharmony and arguments, they find themselves in somewhat of a dilemma.

If you find yourself in such a dilemma it is worth

sitting him down and explaining to him what is bothering you, he may not understand you but at least he will know where you are coming from.

While I have your attention there are three absolutely cardinal rules you must under all circumstances bear in mind unless you have a desire to press the "self destruct" button any time soon:

1. You must not, under any circumstances, get pregnant, and
2. You will not leave any evidence, and
3. If your moral dilemmas prevent you from having fun it's time to get out!

1. It is blatantly obvious to everyone that getting pregnant by a married man is a disaster of the highest order, so however careful you are usually, double your efforts and never ever, ever, under any circumstances, take any risks. Getting pregnant by a married man by accident is reckless, careless, and will more likely than not ruin your affair, and quite possibly at least part of your life. Don't risk it.

Getting pregnant by a married man deliberately or recklessly is even worse, and an indefensibly horrid thing to do. Don't even think about it in your wildest dreams. If you actually want a child find a sperm donor or a man who shares your desire, but trying to trap a man by turning him into a father without his knowledge or consent is indefensible in any situation. When the unwitting victim is married it's as close to a hanging offence as I can think of.

2. Not leaving any evidence requires a certain amount of planning and care which can take some out of the spontaneity out of a physical encounter. It is, however, important and not exactly difficult with a bit of thought. Pay attention to the amount of make-up and perfume you wear, and keep your fingernails to yourself. Certain scratches are hard to explain away with tales of having crawled through a hedge backwards for whatever obscure reason, so just don't leave any.

3. Not every woman can handle the guilty feelings that often accompany sex with a man they should not be having sex with. As sex is usually an important part of an affair this can taint or even ruin the whole affair for those who find it particularly hard to live with the role they have assumed. If this is the case it is time to take a very long, very hard look at the situation and to ascertain if being a mistress is really what the woman in question is cut out to be.

- 17 -
This is not a (normal) relationship

As far as facts that have to be faced sooner or later go, this is one you should face sooner rather than later.

It's not really something you don't actually know already, somewhere deep down, where that particular bit of realization sits slumbering alongside "It's not really correct to have an affair with a married man," and "It'll end in tears."

However, it is a fact that deserves to be woken up, examined carefully, understood and accepted before it is laid to rest again until next time. If you ignore it you will regret it at some point, and not facing it will probably either cause your affair to come to an end at a time that is not of your choosing, or you will make yourself quite dreadfully unhappy because you are living a relationship that isn't what you are allowing yourself to believe it to be.

As the official term "extra-marital" suggests, you are "extra." Extra as in "Outside," extra as in "Additional." The official relationship happens elsewhere. Now that relationship may be pretty reasonable, it may be mundane and boring, or it may be dreadful (although you believe him when he describes it as such at your peril).

For all you know it may even be a pretty good relationship (which beggars the question why he is with you in the first place of course).

But he is not, by any definition "your man." He has a wife (or a long term partner), and you can not and should not try to pretend that what is going on between you and him is a sort of parallel universe version (a much better one in your eyes, of course) of "the real thing."

Some men manage to have two (or rarely even more) simultaneous marriages with two homes, two partners, and two lives. That's called bigamy and is illegal in most places and cultures.

What you are having is an affair, and whilst the good bit about this is that it's at least legal, the bad bit is that you have to accept it as such and not try and turn it into a home-baked form of bigamy, just without the legal consequences.

It is only natural that we want to arrange our lives in a way that follows the path we know and understand as closely as possible, maybe with occasional detours to avoid boredom setting in. It is human nature to crave a framework we understand and feel safe in. Once we reach adulthood we have usually learned how to arrange matters so they fit into that framework, and when things start going pearshaped that framework gives us a sense of security and guidance which is quite comforting.

So we tend to try and apply the same rules to our affair that we would apply to a more conventional relationship. That is a mistake and the sooner we accept that what we are engaged in is an affair and not a conventional relationship the better.

When we have an affair we are moving outside our framework, we are in (for us) uncharted territory, and have to find our way anew at every junction, making up new structures as we move along. That is hard work and very unsettling, at a time when we emotionally need the security of something familiar to hang on to the most.

Hence we tend to try and apply the same structures and a similar framework to an affair as we would have done if we were in a relationship, and are invariably disappointed when the affair does not follow those rules and does not fit the framework we have set for it.

It takes a brave (or foolish, or both...) woman to truly embrace that fact and venture forth into a territory where the "here and now" is what counts and everything else has to be made up as we go along.

To start with this is exciting, and, whether we really admit it or not, one of the aspects of having an affair that makes us believe we're onto something really special. Moving outside the usual framework is a way of breaking out. It makes us feel very free, unshackled by convention, and gives us a dangerously seductive sense of escape.

The more trapped we have felt, consciously or subconsciously, in our life prior to having an affair the more easily we are enticed into entering this dangerous secret universe where there is only us and the man we are getting involved with, and where there are no borders other than the ones we draw; nothing to hold on to than each other, no clear picture of "tomorrow" to guide us, and a "yesterday" that is only ours.

There will, however, come the day where we will get frightened by our own bravery, and where we will feel lost rather than free. So we try to turn the affair into a relationship in our own mind, and apply the familiar rules of past relationships to our affair for security and because we subconsciously want to bring some order back into the chaos we created. Chances are that this is where things will start to go seriously wrong. Repeat after me:

"This is an affair, and an affair is not a "normal" relationship."

If you once again allow me to use my own experiences as an example. I am "doing this whole affair thing" for the second time, and because I have "been there, done it, worn the T-Shirt" previously I apply the rules and frameworks from the past affair to the current one, rather than having to try and fit an affair into the framework of a conventional relationship.

I can't actually remember if and how I figured things out the first time round, maybe we never quite left the heady stages of excitement sufficiently to force me to apply any "normal relationship frameworks" to that first affair.

What I do remember is that the few times when I allowed myself to get somewhat confused about the status of my affair were not healthy.

You are (at least the time being) having an affair. An affair is not a "normal" relationship. Remember that.

- 18 -
Guard your heart

*T*his chapter was originally supposed to be called "Do not fall in love with him." When I looked at it again it occurred to me that this would have been an exceedingly silly title considering how little control we truly have over that matter.

Obviously it would be a positively grand idea not to fall in love with a married man, but usually by the time you buy a book to help you through your affair that particular bit of advice is about as useful as suggesting that you ought not to have an affair in the first place.

If the human race was designed to be able to control their emotions to the extent necessary to even begin to follow this bit of advice the world would be a very different place.

If you are one of the people who has at least a degree of control over her feelings please exercise it for your own sake as much as anything else. However, chances are you will not be able to completely steer your emotions in that way, and this fact will make you both vulnerable and dangerous.

Vulnerable because we all know how much it can hurt when we love someone and things go pearshaped, and dangerous because we know equally well what Shakespeare meant when he wrote that "hell hath no fury like a (loving) woman scorned."

With the deceptive 20/20 clarity of hindsight you may one day judge your own emotions rather differently, see where you may have mixed up lust and love, where you may have been led or even manipulated into believing that you were living out a remake of Romeo and Juliet when what was really going on was simply an affair. Little more (yet also no less) than the age-old situation of hormones getting the better of two people who were in the right place at the right time when opportunity presented itself in the right way.

However, even if you can't stop yourself falling in love with him, either because you already are or because there simply isn't an obvious "OFF" switch to the part of the heart that falls in love, you actually *can* guard your heart to a degree.

Doing so requires some reflective thinking, and a hefty dose of realism which many find hard to digest. It is however in your own interest that you at least attempt to do so.

Guarding your heart involves reserving a part of your brain to the piece of information I have repeated again and again in this book, and which you are actually well aware of if you allow yourself to look at it:

It will end in tears

Now for all intents and purposes this does not come as "news" to you. Deep down we all know that someone is probably going to get rather badly hurt in this, and deep down we are also aware of the fact that this "someone" is most likely to be us.

By ignoring this fact and pretending that it doesn't exist we leave ourselves wide open to getting hurt even more when things go pearshaped sooner or later.

Blows we expect, even if we don't dwell on them too often, never hit us as hard or with as devastating an effect as those that we allow to sneak up on us. What that means in practical terms is that we should allow ourselves to look the facts in the eye from time to time. This does not mean that we should let them ruin what we have, quite the opposite. Let's enjoy the affair and make the very best of it.

What it does mean is that we should periodically, and especially when we are in danger of getting totally swept away by the sheer emotion of it all, remember that the man who elicits such strong feelings and may fast be becoming the center of our universe, is in fact a married man who is probably still going to be a married man long after his affair with us has ended.

This may not be the outcome we desire, and if we beat the odds it may actually not even be the actual outcome of our affair, but if we simply assume this to be the case we will probably have a happier affair and, if we are lucky and play our cards just right, avoid the very outcome we are training ourselves to accept.

By guarding our hearts I don't mean we should stop our feelings. I am saying that even when we allow our emotions to run free they must not be allowed to blind us to the reality of our situation.

- 19 -
No Promises / No Demands

Promises within an affair can be dangerous, or pointless, and sometimes they turn out to be both. When you begin an affair with a married man you know deep down what his promises are worth. You may not feel like thinking about it in detail, but at some point that man stood in front of an altar (or a registrar, or a rabbi, or a Buddhist monk for that matter,) and promised, in some form or another, to be faithful. So much for his promises. He probably also promised to forsake all others. You get my drift.

Now obviously for some people the wedding vows are just a part of an expensive ceremony, with as much real long term impact on their behavior as the candles on the cake, but for most they do mean at least something.

By definition this makes any promise from him to you not exactly worthless perhaps, but you should take it with a large grain of salt. He is not really in a position to make promises anyway, short of the one that he will try not to hurt you, and he may well break that one, too.

If he promises to leave his wife, especially when he does so early in your affair, then he probably won't.

Similar to how people who repeatedly announce their impending suicide usually live to a ripe old age, the married man who keeps pledging to leave his wife "when the time is right" tends to be the guest of honor at his own golden wedding anniversary.

There are, of course, exceptions to every rule but for your own peace of mind, and to prevent you wasting years waiting for a day that may never come, you'd be sensible to work on the premise that for at least the foreseeable future things will carry on as they are. If you are happy with this (or can at least live with it without being unhappy) then that is all well and good. If your plans about your whole future are based on his promises you should give yourself a bit of a talking to, as you will probably be disappointed.

As far as your own promises go, the only things you should pledge is that you will not cause all hell to break lose by doing something stupid such as getting yourself caught or telling his wife about your affair. This means during the affair *and* after it has ended.

Don't promise that you will wait for him however long it takes. His is not a prison sentence which you could sit out on his behalf, waiting for his early release for good behavior! There is no such thing as getting out on remand from a marriage.

You can't promise to be still waiting at a point in the possibly very distant future which is completely out of your control. If you do you may still be holding yourself to that promise when you travel to your clandestine meetings on your free pensioner's bus-pass.

If you are the promising kind, promise each other to

always treat each other with respect, and to be honest to each other when either one of you feels that the affair is bringing more sorrow than it adds happiness to your lives. Just as it is fundamentally wrong to let any normal relationship lie fatally wounded without putting it out of its misery, it is cruel to let an affair turn sour and sad once it has run its course.

As far as promises go, this is one you should make to yourself. Promise yourself that you will get out before it hurts you too badly, or ruins your life. Promise that you will never be the woman who looks back at the past few years and says: "How could I have wasted all this time and emotion on that man?"

An affair should be a beautiful memory, one you should look back upon with a smile and with affection, whichever way the cookie crumbles in the end. Promise him, and yourself, that that's how you will want to remember it if/when it ends.

Making demands is something that doesn't fit too well into any kind of relationship, but I'm afraid making demands rarely has a rightful place in an affair.

You can not really demand a thing apart from being treated fairly which should not have to be demanded in the first place but be standard procedure in any kind of relationship. As far as any other demands are concerned: You are the Other Woman and you knew he was a married man at some point during the proceedings.

Therefore, you are in no position to demand that he sees you at any given time, nor do you have any right to demand that he leaves his wife for you – let alone with any deadlines attached.

If you don't like the way things are going for you then tell him. See what, if anything, he can or wants to do about it, or get the hell out of it. But don't issue demands, it is not your place to do so and won't do you any good in the long run.

But don't let him demand that you arrange your life around the way he can fit his affair (i.e. you) into whatever other commitments he has.

As a mistress we tend to have to be flexible, of course, or we will simply rarely get to spend time with him at all. But if you let him dictate the way you organize your life you will find yourself getting increasingly isolated, because you will be forever changing your own plans to fit in with whatever hour he may or may not be able to spare you.

Not only will your friends get increasingly less sympathetic when you cancel a long planned girl's evening out for the 4th time in a row just because he called round to see you at the last minute, you will also lose his respect sooner or later. What is constantly and readily available is not something that tends to be treasured and coveted long term.

Don't be a doormat. You have a life outside this affair (if you don't – Get one!)

- 20 -
How to effectively ruin your affair

When you ask a man what irritates him most about his relationships (past and present) chances are that often words like "whining, whining, bickering, arguing and complaining" will feature quite prominently and high up on his list.

And when we apply that knowledge to the man we are having an affair with then we can safely hazard a guess that one of the things that he does not like about his marriage or main relationship is that his wife indulges in whining, whining, bickering, complaining and/or arguing more than he finds pleasant or acceptable.

What draws a man to his mistress is that the things that upset him in his official life are conspicuous by their absence in their secondary relationship. His Other Woman is his way to escape all the negative aspects of his marriage when he is with her.

So it does not take Einstein to figure out that any Other Woman who displays the very behavior that irritates him about his wife is heading for trouble. If he is subjected to the same kind of hassle when he is with her as he is escaping from *to* her in the first place, what possible incentive has he got to be with the Other Woman?

Yes, obviously she may possibly be younger, prettier, better at sex and more interesting than his wife, but whether he will admit or even realize it himself, eventually he will not want to continue an affair that adds to the negative aspects of his life rather than providing a welcome escape from them.

It would appear to be unfair to expect the Other Woman to be constantly on her best behavior. No, let me correct that – It *is* unfair. But frankly it isn't actually about being on one's best behavior, it is about accepting which kind of behavior is likely to be both pointless and damaging to the affair.

Let's face it, the majority of arguments between a married man and his Other Woman are to do with communication, the amount of time he spends with her, the frequency and quality of contact and the dreaded "Why don't you leave your wife" question.

Usually, when we get into a relationship with a married man we know he is a married man. We do, at least theoretically, understand that this means limited contact (almost always less than we would like), and the fact he goes home to his wife after spending whatever time he has found to spend with us.

So we would do well to remember those facts of life as the affair continues. There is a great temptation to rearrange things in our own minds in such a way that we actually think the affair is a transition towards a proper permanent relationship, or even that the affair *is*, in fact, a proper permanent relationship.

Once we start judging it against those criteria rather than as what it is (an affair) we can easily become discontented because judged by the wrong criteria the affair suddenly falls short of our expectations.

The more discontented we become the more likely we are to start bickering and causing scenes. We start to expect more time to be spent with us, we ask him to leave his wife, we may cry, we may threaten to end the affair, and generally behave in a manner that is unlikely to make him want to spend more time with us because more and more of the precious time spent with us is ruined (for both) by arguments and tearful episodes.

If we can keep a tighter grip on our view of the whole affair, accepting that, at least for the time being and possibly for the duration of its existence, this is an affair, we can avoid spilling out our disappointment over what is actually exactly what we entered into willingly in the first place.

This does not, of course, mean we should be a doormat, or should allow any man, married or otherwise, to treat us with less respect than we deserve.

But constant complaining about the situation we have actually chosen to be in ourselves will not change that situation for the better.

No man has ever been nagged into wanting to be with someone.

No man with any sense will want to be with someone who is constantly complaining and crying over things he doesn't feel he has an awful lot of control over.

Why on earth would any man leave one hasslesome and unsatisfactory relationship for another equally hasslesome one, especially when doing so comes at such a high price as divorce, financial disadvantages, getting estranged from his children, losing his home and more than likely a number of his friends.

If we want a man to feel that all those sacrifices are worthwhile then we have to be a worthwhile alternative to what we want him to give up.

We can effectively avoid ruining a perfectly good affair if we keep an iron grip on our own acceptance that it is an affair, and remember periodically about all the reasons why we love being with that man.

We went into the affair for some pretty powerful reasons (let's face it, no woman in her right mind would start an affair with a married man for anything less than what did, at the time, look like pretty compelling reasons). So why can't we just try and stay in the affair for those reasons, and enjoy it for what it is for now?

If at any point we come to the conclusion that it is no longer what we want, we are totally within our rights to walk away. No, that's not an easy option obviously, but the cold hard truth is that we won't make things any more to our liking by ruining what little time we get with him.

And by not spoiling things we may, accidentally or by design (depending on how devious we actually are) get just what we want, without any of the fights.

If you still can't quite wrap your head around this try a little mental game:

Imagine you are a married man. Your marriage is not good but it's still bearable enough for you to hang on to it for various reasons. And you have a mistress, and occasionally you wonder if maybe leaving your wife and being with the Other Woman would make your life much better in the long run.

Then imagine two types of Other Women, one who is fun to be with, who listens to you, who you feel a close and deep connection with, who supports you and loves you and who makes every meeting special just as you do for her. Or the other version, the one who wastes much of what little time you manage to spend with her complaining, who cries a lot, and demands things you don't feel you can give her right at this moment in your life.

Now ask yourself: Which is the woman you (when you put yourself in the shoes of that married man) are more likely to want to spend as much time with as you can, and which is the woman you might eventually want to leave your wife for?

Need I say more?

- 21 -
Don't even think about it !

*H*and on heart: If you are having an affair and would quite like it to be a little more than "just that" you have probably thought about how it would be if he left her. And once you allow your thoughts to travel that far you may also have toyed with the thought what would happen if his wife found out about you.

You may even have touched on the purely hypothetical possibility of helping things along a little. As long as you did not go any further than that such thoughts are a little disturbing, but no harm has been done. Don't, however, seriously contemplate actually doing anything along those lines.

If you don't take anything else in this book to heart: This bit is absolutely vitally important if you want to spend the rest of your life looking at yourself in the mirror with a shred of genuine self respect.

You must never, under any circumstances, force the issue and tread loose an avalanche of disaster which, once moving, can not be controlled or directed, and will completely mess up the life of everyone in its path.

In fact you have to take my word for it that it will not and can not and absolute never will have an outcome you could possibly want.

There are four possible outcomes to doing such a thing

1)   His wife goes ballistic, kicks him out, and you end up with him. (This is, surprisingly, *by far* the least likely outcome of "D-day.")

2)   His wife declares war on you and won't dream of giving him up, gives him hell instead and he crawls back under the marital duvet and would rather jump off a bridge than go anywhere near you ever again.

3) Either of the above, and after a while, if and when the dust has settled, he and you resume your affair. But the trust is broken between the two of you.

4)   His wife and him split up or stay together, but you will no longer feature in their lives because he won't have anything what-so-ever to do with a woman who acts like that.

Whichever way it goes, you will lose out. If you can't bear to let things carry on as they are then you have to draw a line and split up with him. But don't try to change matters by wreaking havoc in such a manner.

If he decides that he can no longer live a lie, and that he wants to spend his life with you and not with his wife, then it is up to him to bring about the changes necessary to make that happen. If he does not want to do that, or can't bring himself to take that step, then you have the choice to leave things as they are or walk away.

Forcing the issue is *not* an option, it is *not* your place to do so and you will *not* achieve your dream of long term happiness with the man you love by doing so. Just believe me. It is not going to work out the way you would want to.

Apart from the fact that forcing his hand will not endear you to him in 99.9% of all cases; you will most likely not achieve your goal anyway. Yes, you *may* end up with him that way if his wife kicks him out, dirty socks et al, but do you really want to end up with him by default?

At times the need and dream of "having him" to yourself at long last can be overwhelming. But a relationship wants to be built on a mutual desire and decision to be together, "mutual" being the operative word here....

Quite apart from the fact that his wife will probably decide to fight for him, and not be even dreaming of letting you have him, do you really think you can be happy when you have to wonder if he had ever left the safe harbor of his marriage under his own steam if you had not forced matters?

- 22 -

His wife and family....

$\mathcal{A}$ re none of your business!

However tempting it may be, as his mistress you should stay away from his "other" life.

This is imperative for two vital reasons: The first and most important is that you should stay as far away from them as possible for *their* sake. No wife deserves her husband's mistress loitering around the corner, stalking her in the supermarket or driving slowly past her home at night. She may not know about it, but that doesn't make it any more acceptable.

Watching his children come out of school from across the street is not the act of a loving woman who wants to be close to the man she adores, it is borderline psychotic. Stay away!

Of course you also risk your own peace of mind if you let yourself get too interested.

If you accept that he has a life of which you are no part, and never will be, and then file that part away in one drawer of your mind that remains firmly shut at all times you stand a much better chance of them affecting *you* as little as it possible under the circumstances.

You don't *really* want to know what his wife looks like, how she moves, speaks, cooks, or, god forbid, makes love to him. You don't *really* want to know what their garden looks like, how they have decorated the toilet or what beautiful flower arrangements she puts on the table. Let these images invade your mind too much and you'll drive yourself crazy!

If you can make her that shadowy vague persona that has a bearing on your life by being his wife, but who does not directly affect you, it is more likely that you manage to live with yourself and what you are doing in the long run.

In the cold light of day she is nothing to do with you. Unless she is a friend (in which case – shame on you) you do not really owe her anything, you are not the one who is breaking the promises made to her, you are not the one lying to her or cheating on her. She is his wife and therefore his responsibility, the only responsibility you have is to ensure that she does not find out about you because of something you do.

Don't look at photos of her, don't ask about her, and if he mentions her tell him you don't want to hear anything about it. Chances are that what he tells you about his wife will be a heavily edited version of the truth by definition anyway, so why subject yourself to it? You are not a masochist!

You might say (with some justification) that pretending his wife does not exist is nothing more than a cheap coping mechanism, but you are in a situation where any coping mechanism is a good coping mechanism provided you don't actually delude yourself into really thinking that somehow she doesn't exist. It is one thing to avoid thoughts, facts and images which will serve no purpose other than to give you sleepless nights, and quite another to live in cloud-cuckoo-land. As in so many other respects of having an affair the balance to be struck is your responsibility.

So, accept that he *has* a wife and that the roles are divided up in the age-old way of adultery – her – the wife, nothing to do with you – and you, the mistress, nothing to do with her as long as she doesn't find out about you.

If, of course, she DOES find out about you you'll be facing the reality of her sooner than you'd planned in one way or the other, but that is a bridge you can cross if ever you come to it.

I suppose the one advantage of at least knowing what she looks like is so you can avoid opening the door to her should she pitch up on your doorstep one day with steam coming out of her ears.

Should you be unlucky enough to have to encounter her more or less frequently because you and her have common friends, or because she accompanies her husband to business functions you also have to attend, your situation gets considerably more complicated.

You can no longer pretend she doesn't exist in your life, and if you are unlucky you have to watch them together as a couple.

You should avoid situations like this if you can, for your own sake as well as much as anything else, because she is probably no fool. Unless you are an accomplished actress she may, if she has any sensitivity at all, notice that you are behaving somewhat oddly around her. Underestimate a wife's ability to pick up vibes, from her husband or from you, at your peril.

Should you find yourself in the unenviable position of having to spend time with them because circumstances beyond your control force you to do so, keep any direct contact between the three of you to a minimum without making it too obvious. Being seen to avoid someone can be as much of a give-away as following them around like a lovesick puppy. I recently watched two people who had always greeted each other with a broad smile and a peck on the cheek suddenly behave as if they barely know each other. They had started having an affair. If it was that clear to me then it will be clear to others too, so beware!

So if he is, for example, a colleague and you are both at the same business occasion, greet him like you would any other colleague and then make your excuses with a smile and find someone you really have to speak to. Don't stare at them over dinner, but don't avoid him like the plague either. It's a difficult balancing act and once you have mastered this bit you truly are entering the advanced levels of "Being The Other Woman!"

There is only one situation where you actually must pay close attention to his wife, and that is when she has found out about you and comes to confront you.

This is, of course, a nightmare scenario you will have

done your level best to avoid ever happening.

First of all, do not enter into an argument with her. You will not win this, as she has the moral high-ground by definition! You have wronged her, not the other way round, and she has every right in the world to be very, *very* angry with you.

Don't give her any excuses. "But it just *happened*" will calm her down no more than "We could not help ourselves." There is no explanation, no reasoning, really nothing what-so-ever you can say that will make any difference to her. Blaming him may temporarily deflect her anger but isn't the solution either.

Horrible as it is, the only thing you can really do in this most unpleasant of all possible scenarios is to let her have her say, she deserves it! Obviously you don't have to let her go over the top, and you should protect yourself in the unlikely event that she might get physical, but when you started an affair with her husband you must have known that this situation could, one day, arise. Bear it with whatever dignity you can muster, and if it makes her feel better to call you every name under the sun then just take it on the chin....

Don't enter into a discussion with her, and whatever you do, don't volunteer any details of your affair or reasons why you think he was cheating on her in the first place. You may believe that his marriage was really bad, or over in all but name before he even met you. You may have been led to believe that she is cold, or doesn't understand him (yes, *that* old chestnut), but you can not possibly say these things to her without putting yourself into an even more indefensible position than you are in already.

Really the only thing you should say to her is "Please discuss this with your husband." No more.

Once you have been found out and you have been confronted about it by her (poor you...) it would be a wise idea to let things calm down. What happens next is now out of your hands to a very large degree, don't throw fuel into the fire by calling him or getting in touch with him, he will get in touch with you when he can. If he doesn't you know that your affair has come to an abrupt (and at least temporary) end.

Surprisingly maybe, affairs tend to not die after the first or even often the second time they are discovered. Usually a period of silence follows the initial shock, then the wayward husband tends to start contacting his Other Woman again, and more often than not the affair starts all over again.

However, generally things are never quite the same again. Everyone involved is on their toes, the wife is more suspicious, the husband more nervous, and The Other Woman catches herself wondering if it's all worth it more and more frequently.

- 23 -
The Dreaded "D-Day"

_T_ here are events in life that we dread, and which tend to turn out to be not anywhere near as bad as we feared they would be when they actually happen.

With "Discovery Day" the opposite is usually the case. Whatever the Other Woman imagined, it's probably going to be worse.

A great many Other Women either consciously wish for D-Day to come (the least wise will even tempt fate and actively contribute to it) or adopt a "what will be will be" attitude to it. Usually because they want the whole thing over and done with, decided once and for all, with the decision taken out of their own hands.

Most become sick of the secrecy at some point, and the worry that the wife might find out about the affair. So D-Day seems, at first glance and unburdened by experience, a way to end that state of affairs (if you pardon the pun), once and for all. Other Women who have been through a D-Day or two in their lifetime tend to avoid them like the plague, because they have learned the hard way that it falls most firmly under the heading "Most stressful things that can happen to a woman in a lifetime."

Those who are yet to go through a D-Day tend to fall into one of three main categories:

The ones who believe that D-Day will be their gate to eternal happiness with the married man they love, because his wife will turf him out. Or they think that it will cause such a storm that the marriage, which in the eyes of the mistress must have been teetering on the brink of breaking up anyway, will be pushed over the edge and therefore end for good.

Then we have the Other Women who are so sick and tired of hanging in limbo that they wish for a D-Day just to bring about some decision they themselves are unable to make. They are well aware that the result of D-Day could swing either way, but at least it would swing one way or the other and they are usually in an emotional place where anything that takes the decision and need for action out of their own hands would be a relief.

Lastly we have Other Women who are not (yet or ever) in a position where they would actually *want* their married man turning up on their doorstep clutching a bag of hastily packed essentials. Not because they don't love him, but because they are realistic enough to know that at this particular stage of their life and taking into consideration all aspects it wouldn't or could not work out (yet or essentially ever).

Women who fall more or less into the first category are likely to be in for the greatest shock. They are in for that shock because contrary to their expectation the outcome of D-Day is unlikely to be the situation they expect. They tend to be surprised to find themselves cut off from all communication, and learn that rather than turfing him out or letting him go, the wife will take control of the situation, dig in deep and not dream of giving up her husband, her marriage and, let's face it, life as she knows it, to some more or less unknown Other Woman. She will occupy the moral high ground and occupy it well, and if she is smart will occupy it in such a way that the Other Woman becomes the Ex Other Woman faster than she can say "But I thought..." at least temporarily.

Unfortunately this is the point where a great many cheating men suddenly realize what they stand to lose and try everything to save their marriage. Whatever they may have said to their Other Woman prior to being caught, and regardless of whether they may or may not have meant it at the time of saying it, when the chips are down and the shit truly hits the fan most will do whatever it takes to pacify the wife and hang on to their life, their wife, their marriage and their status quo. In real terms this means they will agree to whatever demands their wives will make, the first and most significant from the Other Woman's point of view being "You will promise never to see "that woman" ever again."

And promise they do ....

He will also most likely tell his wife that you meant nothing, that it was only sex, that you seduced him, that he was drunk.... He will cut both the duration and the significance of the affair down to the very bare minimum he can get away with, beg forgiveness, promise to never ever do it again, and agree to whatever terms his wife may think of.

At that stage the Other Women will probably be cut out of all communication, and will only be told that she should not contact him "for the time being" and that he and his wife need to "work things out." She may be asked to support his story regarding the length of their affair and frequency of meetings, and be asked to lie low, either "until the storm has blown over" or permanently. The fact that the majority of affairs tend to be rekindled a while after D-Day is little consolation. Many are dead and buried that way, and even those that are revived are never the same again, as their status quo has changed. Suddenly the Other Woman has seen clearly what role she plays in her married man's life and which way his choice will fall when it comes to the crunch.

Women often wish for a D-Day for the main reason that they want "something" to happen to bring about an end to being suspended a state of limbo. Often they are incapable or unwilling to bring about that change by taking control of the situation (in other words ending the affair under their own steam) and can wind up actually relieved that events beyond their direct control have taken the matter out of their hands. These women stand a reasonably good chance of moving on with their own lives after finding that the men they had fallen in love with have turned their backs on them and stayed in the happy home. They are often the least likely to be enticed back into the ring for a second round of adultery with the same man.

The woman who does not actually actively want or wishes for her married lover to leave his wife (now or ever) is the one who tries her hardest to avoid D-Day as she neither wishes to wind up with him as a full time commitment nor wants the affair to end. Contrary to popular belief not every Other Woman lives the dream of everlasting coupledom with her married man. Many can and do see the affair as something that fulfills a need, both emotionally and sexually, without necessarily having to "lead somewhere." In other words, they enjoy the affair for what it is, with all its highs and lows, and don't want any drama to mess up what they have. They certainly don't want the drama of a D-Day as they won't gain anything from it, and are in a lose-lose situation if it does happen.

Like most events that have the power to really mess up our life, D-days have a nasty habit of hitting us when we are least prepared and when they are most inconvenient. Murphy's Law applies to D-days quite spectacularly. Of course once you understand the true ramifications of D-Day you also understand that there is rarely, if ever, a "good time" to have D-day. Just as there is never a good time to be run over by a bus or struck by lightning. Once you have been through a typical, or, heaven help you, particularly nasty D-day you may wish you'd been run over by a bus or struck by lightening instead. Hell, even both at the same time might have been preferable! The fact is, the longer your affair goes on the greater your chances of it creeping up on you sooner or later, it would pay to be prepared.

Don't, whatever you do, even as much as dream of bringing on D-Day either deliberately or recklessly in the vain hope that it will change your situation for the better. It is most unlikely to do any such thing, and you may find yourself all alone and despised by both your lover and his wife. His wife will despise you for sleeping with her husband and he may well despise you for taking a decision that should, rightfully or at least in his own mind, have been his to take as after all it is his wife, his marriage, and his situation.

We will assume that you did not take matters into your own hand and that you have woken up on D-Day quite unaware of the drama that is about to descend upon your life. What can have been done prior to the event to lessen the destructive impact it will have on all concerned?

It is not the most romantic or cheerful conversation you can possibly have with your married man, and should be kept both short and confined to a "suitable moment" – but it is a conversation that can save much hassle and heartache all round.

Between the two of you, you should play through what would happen if his wife finds out about the affair. You should agree what he will tell her and what you, if you wind up unlucky enough to be confronted by his wife, should be confirming or denying.

In general you should agree that any conversation between his wife and yourself should consist purely of the sentence: "Please discuss this with your husband!"

This does make you an accomplice in his betrayal and duplicity, granted. It also means that you are agreeing in advance to being cast in a role you almost certainly do not want to assume.

The standard set of lies and half truths in such a situation involve the length of the affair being cut down to the shortest starting point his wife will swallow. It is unfortunately also standard D-day procedure to cast you in the role of an insignificant sexual encounter that was initiated by you and of which your married lover was merely a more or less reluctant but powerless participant. Not every woman can handle being cast in that role but if you have discussed it prior to D-day it will be so much easier to bear than if it comes as a shock after the event.

You may find yourself confronted by his wife, in person or remotely (telephone or e-mail.) Both are bad, but if she does confront you it pays to be prepared. Do not, whatever you do, whatever your instincts may tell you, however hurt or angry or disappointed you are, and whatever he may have told you about her prior to D-day, allow yourself to be dragged into an argument or fight with her.

Again, if at all possible you should just say "Please discuss this with your husband" and stick to that.

No matter how she behaves, you absolutely must stay calm. Protect yourself against her becoming physical (unlikely but obviously it has been known to happen) and stick to the story you and he have previously agreed upon (if for some reason the sensible "Please discuss this with your husband!" bit doesn't suffice)

Don't justify your affair to her, there is no justification. Do not try and explain why it happened (there is no point and it's not your place to offer explanations) and do not apologize (she won't want to hear it... at least not at this stage).

If you can, just take what she is saying on the chin, however hurtful it is. She may have the need to vent and you owe her that much, at least.

Let her have her say, confirm the story you and he had agreed upon previously, add as little as possible to the conversation (such as is) and extricate yourself from the situation completely as fast as you possibly can.

Keep your dignity, do not cry, do not argue with her, do not get angry with her. Like it or not she occupies the moral high ground so comprehensively that there is nothing you can do other than get through the confrontation as unharmed as possible and walk away from it (physically and metaphorically speaking) with your head held high.

You should expect a period of No Contact, the duration of which varies from affair to affair, and generally lasts between just a few days and several weeks, sometimes several months.

Usually the married man will get in touch with his Other Woman in due course after D-day, and more often than not the affair does not end there. Some Other Women I have spoken to have "survived" several D-Days, and every time their affair started up again once the initial storm has blown over.

Personally I find it hard to believe that a wife could catch her husband cheating several times, especially with the same Other Woman, and still stay in the marriage. But much to my surprise this seems to be the case more often than not

- 24 -
Will he leave his wife for me?

This is the question that seems to be at the root of most problems between the majority of "Other Women" and their married partner. It is the cause of most break-ups, and the main thorn in the side of affairs the world over.

If I could erase it from the collective mind of Other Women, including my own, I would. It is a toxic question, a pointless one and must be controlled, if it can not be eradicated, at all costs.

Firstly the fact is that the vast majority of married men who find themselves entangled in a relationship with another woman will, when it comes to the crunch, not leave. I have looked at the statistics, and they looked back at me. Dozens of sets of statistics, all basically saying the same thing, with variations depending on the country of origin and the parameters used to compile them. Although I quite frankly doubt that only well under a handful out of a hundred married men who are involved with another woman actually do leave their wife, the percentage of those who do is still very small, and even if you are a hopeful type who enjoys gambling against the odds, in this particular game they are very clearly stacked against you. No matter what he says and promises, and regardless of whether he honestly and truly believes that he is going to walk out of his marriage to seek eternal bliss in your arms eventually: when it actually comes to the crunch chances are he can't or won't be able to go through with it. This does not make him a liar necessarily, the intention may well be there. But faced with the cold reality of stepping over the line between planning and promising and actually doing it, most will take one last look at what they may fully intend to leave behind, and then back away, either until "a better time" comes along (which rarely actually does) or permanently.

Secondly it is a question which is based on a serious, relationship threatening, and completely false premise: That anyone would ever leave anybody for someone else. People do not leave one partner for another. If there is any leaving to be done, then the one doing the leaving must do it for themselves, not anyone else. Ever. If a man leaves his wife and family in the belief that he is doing so *for* someone else it plants a seed for a big nasty dose of resentment, and at some point in the future this may be thrown straight back in the face of the person they allegedly left their former wife for.

Why men rarely leave their wife to be with the Other Woman regardless of what they say and regardless of whether they intend to, is one of the questions asked by Other Women the world over day-in day-out.

Men are statistically less likely to end a marriage than women. The majority of divorces and separations are initiated by wives for whatever reason. Men appear to have a greater willingness to stay in a bad marriage than women, and seek relief from the situation outside the home by either throwing themselves into their work and hobbies, or by having an affair.

In many respects men have more to lose when they end a marriage than their wives. Even in this day and age the financial and social impact of a divorce is more burdensome on the husband than the wife. If they have children then chances are they will remain with their mother, thus restricting the man's access to them should he leave. His financial situation is most unlikely to improve if he leaves his wife, quite the opposite is generally true. In a worst case scenario it can be almost financial suicide to actually terminate the marriage. There may be a home and assets, there is almost certainly a social network that has been built up over the years by him and his wife. All in all there is generally a huge structure of which his marriage is the core and the essence.

He may, when he is with you, or when things are bad at home, say that he will leave his wife. He will probably, if he is an honest chap and worthy of your love, even mean it when he says it. But when push comes to shove, and he comes eye to eye with the reality of what leaving will actually mean, he will probably back away from the decision, deferring it to another day. He will ask you to be patient, to wait, and tell you that he **is** going to end his marriage, just not quite yet. There will be explanations (I am deliberately and carefully avoiding the word "excuses" in this context) as to why it would be wise to wait, and why he can't do it "just yet." At that point the Other Woman often starts to push for a decision, and he promises to take action when "the time is right."

Generally the "explanations" are one or more of the following

    1) The children (if any) need to be older

    2) The house needs to be paid off in order to sort the finances.

    3) His career needs to progress a bit so he can afford to leave his wife.

    4) His family needs to be prepared slowly and carefully for the breakup of his marriage.

    5) His wife needs to be in a better state of health / frame of mind or she won't cope.

    6) His wife needs to get her career on track / back on track to make a separation financially viable.

As time goes by the "right time" never quite arrives, the Other Woman grows increasingly unhappy and impatient, the married man feels pressurized and starts resenting his mistress, she in turn starts picking fights over the issue, gets naggy or clingy, may issue ultimatums and ultimately the relationship gets more and more strained. At this junction of the road the affair may come to an end initiated by either party, or the Other Woman may accept that he will not leave his wife in the foreseeable future or ever, and continue the relationship on that revised basis.

Making the question of whether he will or won't leave his wife a central issue of our relationship with our Married Men is, frankly, the worst mistake we can possibly make. If the whole issue of anyone leaving anybody else could be taken right out of the equation then more Other Women would actually wind up seeing their married lover leave his marriage to be with them, not less, and the rest would have far happier, far more fulfilling relationships even if they do not end with a "and they lived together as man and wife happily ever after" scenario in the end.

The cold hard reality of the matter is that when we first start seeing a married man we know he is married. We know that the path we are taken is not the conventional route of courtship, dating, engagement, wedding followed by "happily ever after." He's married; we know that, we still start a relationship with them.

So why can't women simply accept what they have, and what they have chosen, and enjoy it for what it is? A relationship that has its restrictions, undoubtedly, but is also usually one of the most intense and exciting relationships that we have ever had. The two facts are linked actually, and we have to be careful to guard our hearts against mistaking the heady mix of secrecy, adrenaline and lust, spiced up with a bit of guilt and a dose of "naughty" for the basis of a solid normal relationship.

There are many, many very happy women who are in relationships with married men for years. Sometimes a lifetime. They tend to have one thing in common, those "Happy Other Women!" They are either not waiting for, or have given up waiting for their lovers to leave their wives. They have accepted things as they are and are living their relationships to the full, within the confines of what it is. A separate entity, in its own right, with its own rules, advantages and disadvantages.

They are not wasting what could be a wonderful love affair (it is not called a "love" affair entirely without justification) by making it a mere state of limbo on the path of what they really want.

If you want a relationship that is free of the constraints that an affair brings, and that has half-decent odds of bringing you into the imagined haven of married bliss, then don't pick a married man to give you that. It may get you there, but that's not the most likely outcome.

If you don't want to waste weeks, months or years staying in a relationship that isn't what you want, however much you may love the man, then get the hell out of an affair with a married man. It's not for you.

But – if you love that man enough, and if you can see yourself wanting to carry on loving him for the foreseeable future, then put the whole concept of "Will he leave his wife for me?" either completely out of, or at least right to the back of your mind.

It has got to be worth it for you as it is: A love affair, no more but certainly no less, or you will be heading for inevitable pain, disappointment and resentment somewhere along the way.

There is little to nothing you can do about his marital status, so you have some choices: You can accept it and make it the best relationship you can, and see where it leads you, making the journey the goal. Or you can end it and find a man who is at least in the position to give you what you desire.

If you can't control or change the situation you have chosen (!) to be in, you can at least try to change and control your attitude to it. If you believe that the only acceptable outcome of your affair is to end up with that man leaving his wife and setting up a new life with you, you will poison what you have and should seriously consider ending it to spare both of you what will most likely happen.

But if you are willing to give the two of you a chance of happiness and your love affair a chance of succeeding as what it is, you could be in for the love affair of your life, something that you can, one day, look back upon with affection and love and a sense of "It was worth it." And who knows, the less you expect him to leave his wife the more likely you are to put pressure on him. The happier you are in your relationship as it is, and the more you appreciate it, the more likely you are to be a woman that he will love, and want to be with. And you could just find that by giving up the quest for becoming "The" Woman in his life rather than "The Other Woman" you could be facilitating just that.

He might just leave his wife, and you might just make it as a "regular couple," and you might just end up where you saw yourself at the beginning of that journey. But don't ruin the journey by making this issue the be-all and end-all of it. Because whatever the outcome may be, the time between the beginning and the outcome will be what you'll remember in years to come, and it would be horrendously bitter to judge it all "wasted" just because, try as you might, you couldn't beat the odds, and ruined what little chance you may have had of doing so by trying just too hard.

- 25 -

The concept of "making him leave his wife"

All too many Other Women spend a lot of time, energy and emotion on trying to work out how they could make the man they are involved with leave his wife.

I have come to the conclusion that there is absolutely nothing we can do to make a man leave his wife. It's something he needs to want to do, something he needs to *need* to do, for himself, first and foremost. There are men who will leave their wife, and there are men, who, despite their promises and despite probably even believing that they will do it, never ever will.

Women are much more ready, strangely, to leave a bad relationship, either to be with someone else or just to be out of a relationship they no longer wish to be in. Far more women initiate divorce proceedings than men, and far more women are the ones to say "Enough is enough, I want and need to get out of this."

Men are more reluctant to get out of even a bad relationship, and close their eyes to reality far more. Men are also more given to procrastination when it comes to relationships.

The realization that there is nothing we can do to

make them take that step is a bitter pill to swallow. But the sooner we swallow it the sooner we can move on – either within the framework of what we have, or away from it completely.

Having said that, it is also my absolute firm belief that whilst we can not make him leave, there are 1000 and 1 things Other Women can do, and do do, that effectively prevent him from leaving.

The statistics which predict that only 3% of married men leave their wife and end up happily and permanently attached to the woman who was the Other Woman, do not mean that only 3 % belong to the type that leaves and 97% belong to the type that does not.

It means that there are a lot of women out there who effectively prevent their married lover from doing the very thing they desire. In other words, amongst those alleged 97 % that see their dreams of "happily ever after" or at least "happily for the foreseeable future" are a good few who tried to "make" their married lover leave his wife, and, in going about it the wrong way, effective blew it.

To understand what may make him leave we first need to understand what made him start an affair in the first place. What was it that drew him to the woman he is having the affair with? And what is it about her, about her behavior, about how she makes him feel when he is with her, that is in such stark contrast to the relationship he has with his wife?

More often than not it is not the obvious, i.e. sex and beauty (they may have ignited the initial spark, but they will not, by themselves, keep the fire burning). The Other Women will probably have shown him that she adores him, that he is fun, will have been fun to be with.

At home there may have been friction, arguments over domestic matters, unhappiness blamed on him, nagging, hurtful remarks, and demands on him he may be finding hard to fulfill and resent.

So when, after a while, his Other Woman begins to display similar behavior to that which made him turn away from his wife, his choice becomes much simpler!

He stands between two situations, and he is being pushed to choose: One he does not have to get proactive about, which may not be a very happy situation but at least it is one he is secure in, knows and understands. There are aspects that make him unhappy, such as the atmosphere, the lack of affection and respect, and the nagging, whining, and the demands.

The other is the great unknown, which would require major upheaval to be chosen, and, also has aspects which cause him unhappiness, ironically very similar to the ones which pushed him away from his wife.

Confronted with two situations that cause him unhappiness as a choice, our average man will do one of two things, he will either just let things be as they are until one or the other situation resolves itself (the Other Woman will get fed up with waiting and end the relationship) or he will choose "the devil he knows." In other words he will stay in his marriage as the alternative is both too hard to choose and not tempting enough to do so, since it has acquired many of the negative factors of his existing life anyway.

During the many, many conversations I have had with both Other Women and men who had affairs, those who left their wife and those who did not, the overwhelming majority of "happy ends" as desired by "The Other Woman" came about without any pressure, and usually relatively unexpected. The women who did end up with their married lover and are still together some time after the event stayed well clear of excessive demands, neediness, and ultimatums. Whether they did so deliberately or subconsciously, it worked for them. As a matter of fact, it worked, for me, as well.

The easiest way to understand this is by removing oneself from one's own situation and looking at the whole concept with a bit of distant realism: Given the choice between an unhappy situation and an unhappy situation – which will the average human being choose? The unhappy one he's already in. Why go through the emotional hell of a separation to end up with something not that dissimilar to what's already been proven not to work? What exactly would be the incentive?

However, given the choice between an unhappy and a happy situation, the incentive to choose the happy situation is at least clear.

Even then there are many men who will never leave their wife, especially when there are children involved. They may say that they will, and more often than not they will honestly believe it when they say it. But when push comes to shove they can't bring themselves to do it. And these men may be in the majority.

However, the rest of the men who, despite declarations of intent, never leave their wife are the ones who might well have taken that step, and may have sacrificed their marriage for a new life for themselves, on the side of the Other Woman.

But the Other Woman blew it, simply by making his choices less easy. Or easy... depending on how you look at it. The idea that "love will conquer all" is all fine and dandy, but the reality is that such an enormous decision as throwing away a marriage and going through the emotional upheaval and financial implications of a divorce needs a hell of a good incentive to come about.

Sadly (or luckily, again depending on how one looks at the whole scenario), there are no tricks to entice a man to leave. There are no methods, no strategies. Not active ones, anyway. But whilst we can not make him leave, we can try not to blow it.

We can try and offer him the kind of situation that he will find easier to choose over the one he is in.

It's not easy, but then we did not end up in a relationship with a married man because we treasure the easy life. It's a choice we made and we can live with it or get out.

If this man is really the one you want by your side all the time, accept that you can't do a thing to make him walk away from the life he already has. Other than making his choice a clear, and pleasant, one. And you *can* control the urge to go and blow it completely by trying to force his hand. Just bear that in mind whenever the urge to pick a fight over anything with him overcomes you. Look at his choices, and understand how you can influence them.

By not being one of the many women who blow their chances.

This is very much not a "How to make a married man leave his wife" book. Because we can not make anyone leave his wife if that isn't what he decides to do.

However, we can avoid actually preventing him from doing so very effectively. The behavior that spoils a perfectly good affair is the same that blows our chances of him ever leaving.

- 26 -
And what if he DOES leave his wife (for me)

First we should take a look at that often uttered sentence "He left his wife for another woman!"

Chances are, when a man leaves his wife he does not do so "for someone else," he does it for himself. This is an important concept to understand, as understanding it fully will have a significant effect on the chance of you two making it as a "normal" couple.

If he left her and is now with you he must have done it for himself, not for you, and not "against" his wife.

It has been mentioned again and again throughout this book that the chance of him ever leaving his wife to start a new life with his Other Woman are pretty small. The odds are stacked against it happening any time soon, and they are, to be honest, stacked against it happening, full stop.

We have discussed how we can cope with that fact and how it should not let us ruin what we do have, that we can have a wonderful love affair with a man whom we adore and who loves us too if we're lucky. We've looked at how we should live for the here and now, and put the question of anyone leaving anybody else for us right out of, or at least right to the very back of our minds.

But... the fact is that however stacked against us the odds may be, and however we should not let the thought rule our mind or the day to day reality of the relationship, we may just find ourselves in the position that life says "Boo to you" to the odds, and we end up in a situation where he does, actually, leave his wife with the clear and unwavering intention of spending the rest of his life, or at least the foreseeable future, with us.

And by not expecting it and not making an issue out of the whole "leaving wife" question we may, more or less accidentally and as a welcome side-effect, have facilitated it actually happening after all.

Amongst the many ladies I have spoken to during the research for this book, the vast majority of those who did end up becoming the sole partner and even wife of their formerly married men were women who did not expect it to happen, and if they did they never pushed the issue with him. They were, by and large, "happy with things as they were" and often mightily surprised (not to say shocked in some cases), when they suddenly found themselves in a situation that they didn't expect. Speaking to men who have left their wives to be with their Other Women the same story unfolded again and again – they were left in peace to take that step without any pressure, in the secure knowledge that their Other Woman was supportive and loved them – but was not spoiling things by pushing and issuing ultimatums.

So, what *if* the odds roll over and die, and you get what you (may or may not have) wished for – His marriage has come to an end either amicably or less so, but it's over and you are suddenly faced with the reality of what was, during the past months or years, even decades, a vague possibility.

You may not believe it, but that is when things tend to actually get difficult. You might see yourself finally getting what you have always wanted, what you have longed for and fought for, and what you truly deserve, a chance to start a new life, in a proper normal relationship, with the man you have loved and wanted for so long.

The old saying, "Be careful what you wish for, you might get it" is never more true than when a mistress gets what she thought she wanted – the man who was having an affair with her.

Depending on the circumstances which led to this new situation you should be prepared for the various scenarios which could develop as a result.

Mostly these fall into one of four main categories:

She ends their marriage without actually finding out about you and him.
She finds out about the affair and throws him out.
He ends his marriage and moves to his own place.
He ends his marriage and turns up on your doorstep with his suitcases.

Believe it or not, the best chances of you and he making it as a couple are afforded by scenarios 1 and 3. Then there is a large gap, followed by scenario 4, and the worst thing that can lead to the end of their marriage from your point of view is scenario number 2.

Why? Well, because he did not end up with you by choice, did not make a conscious decision that his marriage has run its course and that you are the woman he wants to spend his time with from now on. He was forced, the decision taken out of his hands and you wound up with him by default.

Scenario 2 will leave you wondering for the rest of the relationship's life if he would have chosen you given the chance, and if he would ever made that step out of his own free will. These thoughts will probably not invade your conscious mind straight away, you are most likely too busy adjusting to, and possibly panicking over, the completely shifted situation you suddenly find yourself in. But trust me, these thoughts will creep up on you, and depending on your individual make-up they will invade your relationship at future times of discontent and can, if you let them, destroy it.

It won't reassure you if he says that he would have left her sooner or later anyway. You will have heard it all before and the cold hard fact of the matter is, he did not leave her, she got rid of him. You landed yourself with another woman's cast-off. Terrific, just what you always wanted.... Not.

In the middle of a passionate affair we tend to think that him leaving his wife would be the key to everlasting happiness, and absolutely what we want. When a little voice of cold realism occasionally raises its head we usually try not to listen. The grass on the other side of the affair-fence just tends to look way too green.

However, this much longed for situation is, in itself, fraught with problems, and because we don't see them coming in our euphoric state, they tend to hit us harder than they should. So it's best to be prepared for them.

For starters it is unlikely that your married man has been able to extricate himself from his marriage entirely without regrets and sorrow, whatever he may be telling you and believing himself. Few marriages are so bad that their failing does not cause the leaving partner some remorse and a sense of loss and failure.

If he has children this will put further strain on the situation, as their pain will cause their father pain, and often the wife will, consciously or unconsciously, use the children as a weapon against her former husband.

Your life will probably keep its usual base, but his will be turned upside down in almost every respect, and once the initial euphoria has subsided you may well ask yourself what you have got yourself into in much the same way as you did when you started the affair with him.

He will be going through the difficult process of separation and probably divorce, there will be fights with his wife, there will be the inevitable and often negative reaction from family and friends, he will have to deal with lawyers, try to limit the financial implications of his decision and face the question, probably every day, if he has done the right thing, made the right decision.

A man in an exceptional situation such as this is not

the easiest creature to live with at the best of times. And in a situation where not only his entire life has been turned on its head, but your relationship has changed dramatically and beyond all recognition as well, it puts a strain on things that hits people all the harder because it comes as an unexpected extra burden rather than as part and parcel like the usual problems during a time of separation. It is not going to be an easy ride, and the way you both handle those initial months will determine if you make it or not. I have to tell you that again the statistics indicate that the odds of your relationship surviving would make even brave gamblers hesitate to put any money on it.

Essentially you don't really know each other the way most people do before they start a new life together. The way you met and the way your relationship has developed was within the framework of an affair and as such in a somewhat "surreal" setting. Much of the explosive emotional strength was born out of the secrecy and the adrenaline of doing something that would normally be considered wrong. You have probably seen carefully edited versions of each other, having limited time and therefore trying to each be at their best. The secrecy and the danger of the situation has created a strong bond, which now suddenly becomes fragile as the factors that have helped build it have fallen by the wayside.

You may look at each other and wonder what happened to the magic between you. At this point the strain can become simply too much for everyone, and he might be heading back home to give his marriage another chance having found the grass on the other side of the fence maybe greener, but nowhere near as palatable as he may have believed.

If you can make it through the first three or four months you'll probably start steering the whole boat into calmer waters, and how these initial months are approached by both of you will determine the chance you have of making it long term to a great extent.

However huge the temptation may be after all the waiting, it is generally best if he does not move out of the marital home and straight in with you. If it is financially feasible it is almost invariably a much better idea for him to get his own place for the time being.

This will give him a chance to regroup and settle into no longer being married. If he has children it will cause much less hassle than trying to get them used to Daddy moving out and Daddy having another partner all at the same time, and it will avoid enraging his wife any further than she may already be. In fact if she has not found out about your relationship by the time he has decided to leave it may be a good idea to spare her that particular bit of information. If you are, at a later stage, introduced to his family as the new woman at his side your reception is likely to be far more cordial than it could be if you are seen as the reason of the marriage breaking up.

Keeping your true relationship under wraps a little while longer will be beneficial all round in the long run. Assuming you are going to be a couple for years to come it will almost always make an easier and more comfortable story to tell people that you met when he left his wife, or that you were friends during his marriage and fell in love after the split. Most Other Women don't particularly relish the role they played –

and to be cast back into it in the eyes of those around you isn't always the most pleasant experience. Some are rather upfront to the point of being proud of the way their relationship started, but they are in the minority. So wait and keep things on the slow burner for the time being, the rewards will hopefully be worth stretching your patience just that little bit further.

Yes, I know, you have waited patiently for so long (and however long it was, it will seem to have been "so" long) to get to this stage, and will be impatient to at last start that shiny longed for stage of you life and your relationship, but tread carefully. A little more patience now is certain to pay off in the long run, and improve your chances significantly.

You and he will need to get to know each other in a different way now. There are aspects of a relationship which simply can't be practiced during the course of even the longest standing affair. We can compare it to spending wonderful holidays at some destination of our dreams, and then actually going to live there. It is unlikely that there won't be the occasional moment of disillusionment, and a great deal of the magic and the excitement that fed the flames of the affair will die down as the more mundane facts of every day life seep in.

Some of the things that attracted you to each other within the confines of the affair can suddenly become irritants. This, along with the strain of unraveling his married life, heading for and through a divorce, and fighting over assets and access to the children can bring your relationship dangerously close to breaking point.

Stay out of the way of his wife, do not get dragged into any issues regarding his children, gather the last shreds of understanding and tolerance you can find within you when he seems to be unfair to you or becomes distant. You're nearly there now – bite back the desire to argue when it all becomes a little too much, and give the whole thing a chance to settle down before you evaluate your options. All the upheaval that will invariably follow his separation from his wife is another reason to try and not live together straight away. Your honeymoon phase as a proper couple deserves to have a far more pleasant framework, one in which you can rejoice in finally being together. You need a chance to get to know each other in this exciting new stage of your life unburdened from the initial fallout of his leaving.

All the above assumes that is marriage has ended because he has decided to end it, or because he and his wife have mutually, if not amicably, come to an understanding that it is best to go separate ways. There is, however, another scenario which comes with its very own set of problems, and that is when his wife has found out about your affair and has turfed him out, more or less against his will, as a result of your affair.

Even in the rather unlikely event that he seems initially almost relieved to have got out of it without actually having to be proactive about it, the fact that he did not choose his exit will have serious ramifications for your future together.

For starters he will automatically be cast in the role of the bad guy, his wife occupying the moral high ground in all but your eyes. If they have children they may well side with what they perceive, in the innocence of youth, as the injured party: Their mother. Family and friends may see things a little more objectively, but are again unlikely to be a great help at this stage until the dynamics of all the various friendships have been regrouped to take account of the new situation.

Whereas the above effects of him being unceremoniously chucked out of his marriage by a furious wife can be expected and even planned for, the way you yourself react to this unexpected turn of events may surprise you and create problems you had not anticipated.

It is one thing to end up with the man of your dreams because he made the decision to be with you and end his marriages to achieve that objective. To find that he has made no such decision, and to suddenly have another woman's cast-off turn up on your doorstep with no or little warning, clutching a suitcase with some hastily gathered essentials and a shocked look on his face, is another matter altogether.

Maybe you will be initially swept away with the excitement and joy to have him there, with you, finally. But as time goes on, and during the inevitable process of reality setting in, you may not be able to fight off some rather disconcerting questions.

As and when the first wave of events has washed over you, and you come up for breath long enough to survey the way your life has suddenly changed beyond all recognition, you will, sooner or later, have to look some nagging doubts in the eye and deal with them.

The most irksome question that will invade your mind is "Would he have ever left her if she had not kicked him to the curb?" – followed by its insidious little sibling "Did he *choose* me or am I still "The Other Woman" because the "real" one did not want him any more?"

Because by definition you ended up with him by default rather than by his own conscious choice. You will see the fact that you did, in fact, end up with him, as something less bright and shiny, not the great culmination of a love that has deserved to be and was wholeheartedly chosen by both of you. If that question keeps raising its head, and starts to hurt you, you need to bring it up and discuss it with him, hard as it may be.

If you swallow it time and time again and let it fester without addressing it, it could eventually poison your relationship. This stage of your life is going to be fraught with pitfalls that you can not influence or control anyway; it would be most unwise to allow factors you do have some degree of control over to spoil things for you.

Finally, there is one more stumbling block that may or may not become an issue in your relationship: Remember the famous quote from Sir James Goldsmith "When a man marries his mistress he creates a vacancy?" Yes? Well, you may well, at some point or the other, wonder if the leopard has changed his spots, or if he will chat on you sooner or later just as he cheated on his wife with you when you were still having an affair.

There is no simple or obvious answer to that question. On one hand a man who has had an affair before is generally more likely to have another one. However, the more difficult and fraught the end of his marriage before you was, the less likely he is to be tempted to go through the whole thing once again. And if you are smart and manage to carry at least some of the magic that made your affair such an overwhelming success over to your marriage / conventional relationship then he may not feel any need to seek it elsewhere.

You are, at this stage, in the advantageous position of knowing both sides, and you know how he behaves when he is having an affair. Hopefully you have not become complacent now that you "have him", and remember very clearly what led to the two of you getting together in the first place. You should stand a good chance of it not happening again, this time with you cast in the role of the betrayed wife.

And with everything you know now you might just be able to put a stop to it before things get out of hand in the event that he is heading towards another affair. Just never forget all you learned when you were his mistress, those lessons will come in most useful if you do become his next wife.

- 27 -
Coping with "The End"

$\mathcal{S}$ ome affairs are transformed, at some point, into relationships or, more rarely, friendships. Some last for months, years, or decades. In fact the one single fact that surprised me personally most during my research for this book was how many women were, or had been, in a relationship with a married man for as long as they have. Decades in some cases!

However, affairs, like marriages and other conventional relationships, can and do end. They end because they have reached their natural lifespan, and just fizzle out, or they end because one or the other participant decides, more or less reluctantly, to call it a day.

The reasons are as varied as those that lead to the demise of any other relationship, but there are a few factors which, more often than not, bring upon the end more frequently than others, and which are inherently connected to the fact that an affair is not, by definition, like any other relationship.

The man may decide that he can no longer cope with the secrecy and demands that the affair imposes upon him.

His wife may have found out about the affair and forced him to choose, and he may have chosen to stay put (this, incidentally, is usually the least permanent end, as most affairs that end because they were discovered, are revived once the dust in the marital home has settled).

Or the Other Woman may have come to the conclusion that she wants and needs things from a relationship that she can not and will not get from the married man she is involved with. She may well be sick and tired of waiting for him to make a decision, and decide it is better to call it a day and find a man who can commit to her the way she wants.

The relationship may also simply have run its course, with one or both coming to the conclusion that it's just not what they want any more, and end that way.

However it ends, it will almost certainly be painful for both, and especially so for the Other Woman.

I did, right at the beginning of this book, say "It will end in tears, probably yours" – and that holds true especially where the end of the relationship is concerned.

Few relationships die quietly, of old age, in their sleep. They tend to have to be killed, by one or both of the people who were once so in love. And that is unlikely to be a painless or comfortable process. It's hard enough when a conventional relationship comes to an end, but coping with the end of an extramarital one is even harder.

When a conventional relationship or a marriage breaks down, both partners tend to be able to talk about it, will have some support system from family and friends already in place, someone to talk to, and a framework of experience from their own and other peoples' failed relationships to get direction from.

When her affair dies, the Other Woman tends to have comparatively little in the way of support.

By the very nature of the beast her family and friends will be far less supportive or sympathetic towards her – and if she has been a discreet person her nearest and dearest may not even know that she was ever involved with the man who has just broken her heart.

The bad news is: It's going to hurt, and it's probably going to hurt badly. For quite a while.

If we think about it logically there can be no all round "Happy End" to an affair. Someone is likely to get hurt whichever way the cookie crumbles. In the (admittedly rather less likely) event that he does leave his wife then the wife (and he himself to greater or lesser degree) will be hurt.

We really should be quite clear on the fact that someone will be hurt from the outset, so it doesn't come to hit us in the face unexpectedly when the inevitable happens.

The good news is that very few, if any, people die from broken hearts. It just sometimes feels like that would be the preferable outcome. And broken hearts heal, however unlikely it seems right in the middle of the pain. In time you will be ok, and you will find someone else, preferably someone who is free to be with you the way you want and deserve.

There are some ways to prepare for the end, cynical as that may seem, while things are still running their course more or less beautifully. It's the blows that hit us sideways and unprepared that wreak the most devastating havoc, so the wise Other Woman will look the end in the eye before it actually raises its ugly head, and put her support system in place so it is there to be grasped if or when needed.

If you have read this whole book, and taken at least some of the contents on board, you will not be hit by the end as unprepared and devoid of the structures that will help you pull through it.

You will have made sure that your entire life did not revolve around the man you have just broken up with. You will have looked after your existing friendships, and developed some new ones. You will have kept your hobbies going and made sure your career is running smoothly. All those things will help you fill the gap that is opening up with the demise of your affair.

Hopefully you will have one or two sympathetic friends whose shoulders will be available to cry on and who knew about the affair before it drew to an end.

A few words of warning though. However angry, hurt, furious and even desperate you may be over the breakup, you must not now lash out and try to revenge your broken heart.

This is most definitely not the time to cause him harm by making sure his wife finds out just what her husband has been up to.

It may be a natural reaction to at least contemplate such a deed (although I can honestly say it would not be in my own nature, but different people react differently.) This is one temptation that must be resisted under all and any circumstances. Nothing will be gained by it, it would not make you feel any better (just trust me on that one-) quite the opposite, and despite of what you may try to make yourself believe, it would not be an act of sisterly kindness but a vicious, nasty blow to someone's life who has already been the victim of your and his duplicity, albeit without actually suffering from it as she did not know.

The only way to make sure that one day you can look back at this episode of your life with your self-respect still intact is to walk away from the whole thing with you head held high and your pride, dented maybe, but intact.

Cry all you like, mourn the passing of what you had hoped would be the love of your life and what, quite possibly, was just that.

Cry for those broken dreams and shattered hopes and be angry that your future won't be as you had been led to believe, by him or your own imagination or both. But don't do anything that will make things so much worse than they already are (and yes, it *is* possible!) You would only regret it.

Go out, see your friends, have your hair done, take a holiday, find a new hobby, whatever it takes to fill the emotional holes that open up at the end of a relationship, whether it was you who ended it or the man you were involved with.

You may find solace in sharing your story and your pain with others in a similar situation; there are some very good forums on the internet which are specifically for Other Women and their issues. And just believe that you will come through this, eventually, stronger than before, and a little bit wiser. And having learned something from it all.

And if you have done it right you will, one day, look back at the whole affair and not regret it. For all the pain of the end you will not see it as a waste of time and emotions. You will see it as an episode of your life, a great love that, ultimately, was not to be, but that was wonderful while it lasted.

That is what I meant much earlier when I said:

"Make memories that count. One day those may well be all you are left with."

- 28 -

"Ooops, I did it again...."

Having another affair (or two, or three....)

*M*ost women who had an affair with a married
man will, after it ended, be quite certain they
won't go there again. They may change their mind
when they meet the right man, but usually the end of
an affair finds a woman quite certain that they will,
from this day forward, stay as far away from married
men as they possibly can

A great many men, having got away with an
extramarital affair once, will stray again after that first
affair has come to an end.

Why is that so? From the many conversations I had
on the subject with men and women who have had
affairs (note the plural) and women who were involved
with married men the overwhelming impression is that
men and women see the ended affair differently.

It would appear that women tend to think of it as
something unique, something they "would not
normally have done," and something that can't be
replicated by just picking another married man.

They also have the choice of picking a single man as
their next partner, whereas the married man can either
return to the monogamy of his marriage or chose

another woman to have an affair with.

Women also tend to remember very clearly and sometimes overwhelmingly the pain of the affair ending, rather than the good bits of the affair while it lasted.

Men, on the other hand, appear to remember and miss the good aspects, yet not always necessarily as much the person they experienced them with.

While women miss the person first and the "nuts and bolts" secondly, men frequently miss the actual affair more than the Other Woman themselves.

Men are very aware of the fact that they "got away with it" (provided they did). They got away with it once, so it gets easier to start a second affair. They got away with it twice or even more often and every time starting another affair gets easier as the fear of getting caught and the ramifications that would follow subsides.

That is how serial adulterers are made, by a process of getting away with it repeatedly.

Unfortunately men who have learned that they can have their cake and eat it over the course of several affairs are the least likely to ever actually leave their wives under their own steam. They have usually become complacent, and regardless of how much they may care about their mistress they have learned from experience that another one will come along should this affair fail for some reason.

This also means they are more likely to end an affair when it becomes hasslesome. In fact the only type more likely to run for the hills at the first sign of trouble is the first time offender who did not actually "want" to have an affair, and is of an anxious disposition.

So why do women have another affair with a married man when really they remember all too clearly that it didn't work out the way they wanted the first time round?

Obviously some women are simply unlucky enough to fall in love with another man who is married. It could be argued that the first time it may have been an accident, but when they came across the choice for the second time they really should have known better.

But if we applied that logic to relationships in general people would only ever have one relationship, as the end of this might have told them that relationships in general don't work.

And hope springs eternal, despite the quote:

> "Insanity is doing the same thing again, yet expecting a different outcome"

I don't actually subscribe to this quote, because often we have to do things a few times, each time learning how to do it better, before we get it right.

But is there a way to "get it right" when it comes to affairs? Are they not, by definition, wrong?

Yes, in many ways having an affair is wrong, and we are in no real doubt about the fact that they are.

But for many women, if they admit it to themselves or not, unavailable men become a major magnet.

It is usually a combination of the sheer thrill of doing something that is forbidden, alongside an often unconscious unwillingness to really have a fully committed relationship.

Sometimes an affair simply fits into a certain stage of a woman's life. A woman may usually want a proper full-time relationship, but go through times when this simply wouldn't be what she wants or needs temporarily.

So by having another affair, hopefully with the pitfalls of the previous one still firmly in her mind, she can, put bluntly, have her cake and eat it.

Much is said about men who have affairs being "cake-eaters," but frankly the concept of "having it all" does not just apply to the man. In fact the man has more to juggle, and ultimately more to lose, than the woman he is having an affair with.

My own situation is slightly different to many: My first affair was almost entirely very happy, there are no regrets and nothing that could really have implanted a "Never again" thought firmly into my consciousness. Maybe that is why I entered another one with comparatively little misgiving.

I am slowly but surely learning about some of the pitfalls I missed out on first time round, but I still can not bring myself to regret it. The last word has not been spoken though and I may find much to regret about it if and when it comes to an end.

But for the time being I am a happy "Other Woman."

Will I ever do it yet again?

I doubt it. "Never Say Never" as they say, but as I grow more sensible I can see that next time (if there is a next time) I fall in love with a man I will want him to be someone who can be with me a little more freely. Hopefully someone who could, if we both choose to do so, live with me and be there for me the way I am there for him without having to look over our shoulders the whole time.

I have to admit, however, that there are aspects of having an affair that I would probably always miss, at least a little bit, and at least some of the time.

We have looked at the fact that adrenaline and a sense of "doing something forbidden" is a powerful aphrodisiac.

The way we still get butterflies in our stomach when the man we are having an affair with calls or comes through the door, even after quite some time and when a normal relationship will have become much more "routine," is very seductive.

Some women suddenly realize that much of the excitement is caused by having an affair first, and the person they are having the affair with second. This realization can tempt us to replicate the emotional highs by having another affair.

Amongst the people I have spoken to were many serial offenders. People who had more than one affair, some actually being on their 5th or even 10th.

Most were not quite sure what drove them back onto the rollercoaster repeatedly, and few actually recognized the reasons for this pattern in their lives.

Generally I would suggest that once we have realized that having an affair is unlikely to be the easy path to "happy ever after" we should try and stay away from doing it again.

But... "Hope springs eternal" as they say, so this particular piece of advice, however sensible it may be, is unlikely to talk us back from the edge when we are presented with another married man that catches our attention.

- 29 -

Quotations for The Other Woman

ଔ

It is better to be unfaithful than to be faithful
without wanting to be.
Brigitte Bardot

ଔ

Never be unfaithful to your lover except with
your wife.
Satchel Paige

ଔ

Adultery is the application of democracy to love.
Henry Louis Mencken 1880 – 1956

ଔ

Four things does a reckless man gain when he
covets his neighbor's wife – firstly demerit,
secondly an uncomfortable bed, thirdly,
punishment and lastly, hell.
Seneca – 1st Century AD

ଔ

I have looked on many women with lust, I have committed adultery in my head many times. God knows I will do this and forgives me.
Jimmy Carter – 1924 -

ᘓ

Nothing is more pleasurable than to sit in the shade, sip gin and contemplate other people's adulteries, and while the wormy apple of marriage still lives, the novel will not die.
John Skow

ᘓ

Women react differently: a French woman who finds herself betrayed by her husband will kill his mistress; an Italian will kill her husband; a Spaniard will kill them both; and a German will kill herself.
Bernard Le Bovier Fontenelle – 1675 – 1757

ᘓ

Adultery usually follows a law of diminishing returns.
Anonymous

ᘓ

It is easier to play around with a man's wife than with his clichés.
Tom Robbins 1936-

It is easier to play around with a man's wife than
with his clichés.
Tom Robbins 1936-

Do you seriously expect to be the first Prince of Wales in history not to have a mistress?
Prince Charles – Prince of Wales

Horses for ye, and brown Greek manuscripts, and mistresses with great smooth marbly limbs.
Robert Browning – 1812 – 1889

Nay but you, who do not love her! Is she not pure gold, my mistress?
Robert Browning – 1812-1889

Much can be inferred about a man from his mistress: in her one beholds his weaknesses and his dreams.
Georg Christoph Lichtenberg- 1742 – 1799

The first breath of adultery is the freest; after it, constraints aping marriage develop.
John Updike

CR

Passion is the evil in adultery. If a man has no opportunity of living with another man's wife, but if it is obvious that he would like to do so, and would if he could, he is no less guilty than if he was caught in the act.
Saint Augustine

CR

As a musician I tell you that if you were to suppress adultery, fanaticism, crime, evil, the supernatural, there would no longer be the means for writing a single note.
John Bizet

CR

No adultery is bloodless.
Natalia Ginzburg

CR

≈

A lover always thinks of his mistress first and
himself second; with a husband it runs the other
way.
Honore de Balzac

≈

If ever a man and his wife, or a man and his
mistress, who pass nights as well as days together,
absolutely lay aside all good breeding, their
intimacy will soon degenerate into a coarse
familiarity infallibly productive of contempt and
disgust.
Lord Chesterfield

≈

Next to coming to a good understanding with a
new mistress I love a good quarrel with an old one.
George Etherege

≈

We often choose a mistress as we do a friend –
for no particular excellence in themselves, but
merely from some circumstance that flatters our
self-love.
William Hazlitt

≈

❧

Even a most faithful mistress can be bent by
constant threats.
Sextus Properius

❧

Men will bear many things from a mistress
which they would never bear from a wife.
Samuel Richardson

❧

The more a man loves his mistress the more he
is ready to hate her.
Francois de La Rochefoucauld

❧

The man who thinks that he loves his mistress
for her own sake is mightily mistaken.
Francois de La Rochefoucauld

❧

No lover, if he be of good faith, and sincere, will
deny that he would rather see his mistress dead
than unfaithful.
Marquis de Sade

❧

❧

A mistress should be like a little country retreat
near the town, not to dwell in constantly, but only
for a night here and there.
William Wycherley

❧

I could not stand that my husband was being
unfaithful. I'm Raquel Welsh – understand...?
Raquel Welsh

❧

I do not think that there are any men who are
really faithful to their wives.
Jaqueline Kennedy Onassis

❧

Divorce is the sacrament of adultery.
French Proverb

❧

You know that the Tasmanians, who never
committed adultery, are now extinct.
Maughan Vaughan Somerset

❧

❧

University degrees are a bit like adultery: You may not really want to get involved with that sort of thing but you don't want to be thought incapable.

Sir Peter Imbert

❧

Mistresses are like books: If you pore upon them too much, they doze you and make you unfit for company; but if used discreetly, you are all the fitter for conversation by them.

William Wycherley

❧

Next to the pleasure of finding a new mistress is the relief of getting rid of an old one.

William Wycherley

❧

It is easier to keep half a dozen lovers guessing than to keep one lover after he has stopped guessing.

Helen Rowland

❧

ᘓ

Matrimony isn't a word, it's a sentence.
Anonymous

ᘓ

Never let your sense of morals prevent you from
doing what is right.
Isaac Asimov

ᘓ

A woman should say: "Have I made him happy?
Is he satisfied? Does he love me more than he
loved me before? Is he likely to go to bed with
another woman?" If he does, then it's the Wife's
fault because she is not trying to make him happy.
Barbara Cartland – Novelist – 1901 –

ᘓ

Jealousy is a painful passion that passionately
seeks what causes pain.
German Proverb

ᘓ

When a man marries his mistress he creates a
vacancy.
Sir James Goldsmith

ᘓ

❧

Money differs from an automobile or mistress in being equally important to those who have it and those who do not.
Unknown

❧

When we are tired of loving, we are quite content if our mistress should become unfaithful as it loosens us from our responsibility of fidelity
Unknown

❧

You are my lover and I am your mistress, and kingdoms and empires and governments have tottered and succumbed before now to that mighty combination.
Violet Trefusis

❧

A deaf husband and a blind wife make a happy couple.
French Proverb

❧

❧

Bigamy is having one wife too many. Monogamy is the same.
Oscar Wilde

❧

A lady is nothing very specific. One man's lady is another man's woman; sometimes, one man's lady is another man's wife. Definitions overlap but they almost never coincide.
Unknown

❧

A lover without indiscretion is no lover at all. Circumspection and devotion are a contradiction in terms.
Unknown

❧

Do not envy a sinner; you do not know what disaster awaits him.
The Bible

❧

Moral indignation is jealousy with a halo.
H.G.Wells

❧

CR

My wife's jealousy is getting ridiculous. The other day she looked at my calendar and wanted to know who May was.
Rodney Dangerfield

CR

Plain women are always jealous of their husbands. Beautiful women never are. They are always so occupied with being jealous of other women's husbands.
Oscar Wilde

CR

A man in love is incomplete until he has married. Then he is finished.
Zsa Zsa Gabor

CR

The only thing worse than a man you can't control is a man you can.
Jean Kerr

CR

When a man steals your wife there is no better revenge than to let him keep her.
Edgar Watson Howe

CR

႙

Eighty percent of married men cheat in America.
The rest cheat in Europe.
James Holt McGavran

႙

When I can no longer bear to think of the victims
of broken homes, I begin to think of the victims of
intact ones.
Ken Dodd

႙

Seduction isn't making someone do what they
don't want to do. Seduction is enticing someone
into doing what they secretly want to do already.
Waiter Rant

႙

It is not love that is blind, but jealousy.
Lawrence Durrell

႙

I was not kissing her, I was whispering in her
mouth.
Chico Marx

႙

ભ

My twin passions, homeopathy and infidelity.
Charles, Prince of Wales

ભ

Men marry women in the hope they will never change. Women marry men with the hope that they will. Invariably they are both disappointed.
Albert Einstein

ભ

In modern usage a cocuckold is the husband of an unfaithful wife – a far nastier and more humiliating state, apparently, than being the wife of a philanderer, for which in fact no word even exists.
Anne Fausto

ભ

When love becomes laboured we welcome an act of infidelity towards ourselves to free us from fidelity.
Francois de la Rochefoucauld

ભ

- 30 -

"What a wicked web they weaved"
A case study

The Story of S, H, R and assorted supporting ladies

While this story was unfolding before my eyes I thought it was something completely extraordinary, something that did not happen all over the world and has been happening in various guises across the centuries. I was wrong.

Let us have a look at the leading roles. S was a seriously nice girl, from a great family, who went to the best public schools, a very pretty blonde with the right career in advertising, a nice little house in a semi rural area outside London, a couple of good horses and an active social life.

Then she met H, and fell in love with him. Unfortunately H was, at the time, married with 2 semi-grown up kids and a thriving cash-rich company to boot.

H and S started what they called a relationship, and the outside world would have called a sordid affair had they known about it. H was no stranger to extra-marital activities, but with S it was different. She fitted his growing status as a successful businessman much better than wife No. 1 and instead of indulging in a One-Night-Stand or short fling as usual, he and S soon became an item, both convinced that this was "the real thing."

This was S's first expedition into the land of adultery, and like almost every other woman who falls in love with a married man S was quite convinced that her situation was unique, that this was not just yet another illicit affair and that their love, such as it was, was destined to conquer everything for eternity.

H eventually left his wife, and the resulting mayhem did not have the commonly anticipated detrimental effect on his relationship with S. Quite the opposite happened, it pushed them even closer together.

Whilst assorted family, friends, neighbors and the local gossips at their favorite pub were still pouring over all the salacious (and mostly inaccurate) details of this latest scandal we watched H secretly and quietly hide away assets both from his company and his personal accounts. Vehicles were re-registered in various names, company books were "edited" and company assets vanished. By the time the fertilizer hit the fan he looked like an (admittedly very well dressed) pauper in a brand-new Range Rover that had been cleverly registered in someone else's name.

H's first wife had been too busy complacently enjoying a life that concerned itself mainly with running the household, bringing up the kids, partaking in village activities and the Pony Club. As a result she was ill equipped to either foresee or prevent what her soon-to-be ex-husband was up to, and by the time she finally woke up and smelled the coffee it was way too late.

H had diminished his worth on paper to near the poverty line, and with the help of an inventive accountant and a lawyer who was unafraid to skid along the edge of legality and way beyond, had managed to make himself look virtually penniless.

Considering the enormous care he had taken to end his first marriage in the most financially advantageous manner for himself, it is surprising how little foresight he showed at the time regarding the possibility of his second marriage (which was, at that stage, not even on the cards of course) failing. It would, in due course, prove to be a fairly expensive mistake on his part to have let "S" in on a lot of the details of his, let's call it "inventive" accounting. Being the smart lady that she was she did not forget a lot of it and when, many years later, this relationship imploded with a bang, she used what he taught her against him with both intelligence and a rage that surprised everyone.

Anyway, at the time it all went swimmingly S's way, and if the manner in which H ended his first marriage had started any warning bells ringing in her head she either could not or did not want to hear them.

She was too busy working on this great new life she and H had planned and trying to re-build the bridges between herself and her family, who were none too thrilled at the prospect of this newly divorced potential son in law, and most concerned about the damage to the family reputation.

S was undeterred by her mother's repeated wails that this was the first whiff of scandal to have touched their family since the reign of Elizabeth the First, and stuck firmly by H's side. They bought some land and started building up a farm, using all available tricks to obtain planning permission. S gave up her job and became a (admittedly rather fancy and well dressed) farming lady while H carried on running his company to finance their grand plans.

By the time their house was starting to be built the cracks in their relationship had already started to widen to the size of small canyons, H was up to his old tricks again but S, who had, after all, been his mistress before becoming his second wife, was not as innocently trusting as Wife No 1 and had smelled a rat long ago.

Unfortunately for her, like all things he did H did not conduct his affairs without planning their execution much like he did his business deals, and covered his tracks very well. Obviously S had a distinct advantage over H's first wife in that she knew a lot of his tricks, remembering only too clearly how he managed to cover his tracks when she was on the other side of the cheating triangle, and with the pink fog of first love most clearly removed she remembered only too well what to look out for.

Infuriatingly this meant that she sensed that he was up to no good, but not how, when and most pressingly, with whom.

S was my best friend at the time and we spent a lot of time driving around looking for his car in the wrong places and hiding down dark country lanes in borrowed vehicles in the hope to be able to follow him without being noticed. We were soon going through the dustbin, his organizer, his mail, his car and the phone bills in the hope of finding some clue as to the "other woman's" identity and basically behaving like a couple of amateur Miss Marples, with rather mixed success it has to be said.

Mostly our efforts were quite in vain, H was smart and careful, and by nature a coldly calculating type so no matter how ingenious our ploys, he was usually one step ahead of us.

The fact that he changed his mistresses as frequently and unpredictably as he changed his tactics also meant that all too often, just as we were getting close, he would dump the current object of his affection and move on, cleverly leaving them in such a way that he got rid of them without inciting their anger and thus risking their revenge.

Just as things looked ready to fall apart completely S fell pregnant, and for a while it looked like the prospect of fatherhood might have caused a change of character in H, he pulled himself together and whilst not quite attaining "model-husband" status he behaved pretty much well enough.

When S gave birth to a daughter they did, for a while, resume what appeared to everyone outside, and probably to them as well, a reasonably functioning marriage.

H doted on his little daughter and absolutely adored her, and held S in a kind of new regard as the mother of his beloved child. You could not, in all fairness, fault him as a father, and like many men who have children with a second partner he became almost a model dad, avoiding many of the mistakes he made when his sons from his first marriage were small.

However, soon the cracks started showing again, and things went both rapidly and dramatically downhill, this time with the child being most passionately fought over.

S began to contemplate separation and no longer cared whether H was cheating on her or not, let alone with whom. She spent more and more time doing her own thing, bringing up her daughter and otherwise concentrating on her horses, the farm and her friends.

One such friend was R, a neighbor also married with a child, who had been at the center of S and H's social circle for as long as anyone could remember.

Now I pride myself on having very finely tuned antennae for interpersonal vibes, be they positive or negative, and yet I never saw this one coming at all until it had already been going on for quite a while. Nor had, at that stage, H. In hindsight it is likely that he at this stage no longer cared much one way or the other whether S was seeing anyone else or not. The violent way he reacted when it all came out had more to do with *who* she was cheating on him with than the fact she was unfaithful in the first place.

It came to an almighty showdown one night, in the middle of a muddy field, which resulted in some black eyes and a broken nose.

If S had in some way conned herself into thinking that H would handle divorcing her any differently than he handled divorcing his first wife she would soon learn that she was gravely mistaken.... If anything, H and his support team had learned from the few loopholes he inadvertently left for his first wife to find and had closed them.

S's advantage of knowing what he did during the course of his first divorce helped her case a little, but she still found herself done out of most of the proceeds of several years of relentless work. She had to stand by and watch quite helplessly how he somehow managed to appear quite penniless yet again, and also how he manipulated the facts until their valuable home, a gorgeous newly built house in a prime location in one of the most expensive areas of the country, with stables and grazing land and within sight of Windsor Great Park, suddenly appeared worth very little, yet just a bit more than she could get her hands on, so he kept the lot. The house, the farm, and almost her horses as well.

She did, after a long and extremely bitter and dirty (not to mention extortionately expensive) court battle, get custody of their child, but all in all she walked away with a fraction of what, if life was fair, she should have had.

Her affair with R did not last the course, he went back to his wife and they are, as far as I know, still together.

H lived alone in the former marital home for a while before marrying again. Last time I spoke to someone local he was once again up to his old tricks and seeing an Other Woman on the side.

S and I sadly lost touch, but I hope she eventually found lasting happiness with a good man.

- 31 -
Mighty mistresses throughout history

"You are my lover and I am your mistress, and kingdoms and empires and governments have tottered and succumbed before now to that mighty combination."
Violet Trefusis

The quote above is an interesting one. All too often the Other Woman in a married man's life tends to think of herself as powerless, as a victim of circumstances, and someone who is living a half-life compared to the man they are involved with, who seems to be getting "life and a half."

However, throughout the centuries, and all over the world, in all cultures, again and again, there have been mistresses who have changed the course of history.

They were strong women, smart women, women who took destiny in their own hands and played their cards just right, both in their private and public life. They were the ones that stepped out of the shadows, held their heads up high, and went for what they wanted. Whole heartedly and bravely. Not always "happily ever after," but still, they are the ones that are remembered, alongside or often more than the men they were involved with, whilst as a rule no-one really remembered the names of the wives they pushed to the sidelines.

There are so many examples, but let us look at some of the most interesting ones, chosen for the brilliance with which they played their cards, and the impact they had on their time and the life of the men they got involved in.

Cleopatra

Arguably the most powerful woman in history, Cleopatra's rise to power came about when her father, Ptolemy XII, died. At the time Cleopatra was about 18 years of age. Along with her 12-year-old brother, and husband, Pharaoh Ptolemy XIII, Cleopatra became co-ruler of Egypt upon the death of her father in 51 BC, assuming control of the empire.

Cleopatra's increasing status amongst the people troubled her brother and husband, and with the aid of the Eunuch Pothinus, who served as regent for the boy-pharaoh, Ptolemy attempted to have Cleopatra deposed. He succeeded in forcing Cleopatra to flee to Syria, where she raised an army, thus beginning a civil war. To make matters worse for Ptolemy, another sister took advantage of the political upheaval and made her own bid for the throne.

During this same time, political strife in Rome had pitted Julius Caesar, who requires no introduction, against his co-consul Pompey Magnus. Pompey, fleeing Caesar's armies, made his way to Egypt in order to seek refuge. Ptolemy XIII pretended to accept his request, but in an effort to win favor with Caesar, who he hoped would support his cause against Cleopatra, Ptolemy had Pompey executed. When Caesar finally arrived in Egypt, the gift of Pompey's head had rather an opposite effect than the one Ptolemy wished.

Cleopatra had somewhat more success with the married general. As the story goes, Cleopatra had herself delivered to Caesar rolled up in a Persian carpet. Charmed by her self-presentation, the married Caesar very swiftly fell for the Queen who, though contemporary portraits suggest she was not traditionally beautiful by modern standards, was, by all accounts, a very accomplished and intelligent woman. Their affair was an open secret, and soon Cleopatra convinced Caesar to support her quest for her throne.

Caesar reinstated Cleopatra to the throne as co-ruler, but this situation did not please her husband/brother. He rallied an army to wage battle with Caesar's and Cleopatra's armies. After a battle that destroyed significant sections of Alexandria, Ptolemy's legions were defeated and the young Pharaoh drowned in the Nile as he attempted to flee. Cleopatra took control of the throne, but named her younger brother, Ptolemy XIV as her co-ruler.

The political turmoil quelled, her love affair with Julius Caesar continued. Cleopatra gave birth to his son, Caesarion in 47BC. Cleopatra and Caesarion visited Rome in 47BC and 44BC, and may have been present in the city at the time of Caesar's assassination on the Ides of March, 44BC.

Upon Caesar's assassination Cleopatra, who

suddenly found herself without her powerful ally and lover, sought out and found another world leader worthy of being the man on her side.

That man was Mark Anthony, and for the next 12 years they ruled their empires with great success. The relationship produced twins before Mark Antony and Cleopatra married in 36BC, and another son, Ptolemy Philadelphus.

It would appear that all that power went to their heads at some point, and Antony and Cleopatra, self-styled gods, greatly displeased Rome. Octavian, one of the triumvirs of Rome, declared war on Egypt.

Cleopatra and Antony raised their armies to fight against the Roman war machine, but following a major naval defeat at Actium in 30BC, Antony, believing Cleopatra to have already killed herself, fell on his own sword.

Allegedly, Cleopatra, now aged 39 and used to being the mistress of the most powerful men of her time as well as the wife of complete weaklings, tried to seduce Octavian, with the intention of repairing the relationship with the Roman Empire. Octavian, however, planned to overthrow Cleopatra by completely humiliating her in the eyes of the world.

His plan was to take her back to Rome and to parade the, now powerless, Empress of Egypt through the streets for the edification of the mob.

Aware of Octavian's plan, Cleopatra, an immensely proud women, exerted her power one last time. Rather than allowing herself to be captured and humiliated, killed herself with the help of a poisonous snake.

The Marquise de Pompadour

Probably the most famous royal mistress in Europe, certainly in France, was the Marquise de Pompadour.

France has always had a far more open and practical attitude to royal affairs, accepting that most marriages are political instruments, a consolidation of wealth, power and land that often led to the formation of dynasties and connections of States.

These unions were rarely, if ever, considered a true match of loving hearts – in fact the idea of a love match between elites would have struck contemporaries as a peculiarity at best and a political liability at worst.

In France the King was almost expected to have affairs, and the main "maitresse" was even awarded her own title of *"maîtresse en titre"* and held in generally high esteem by everyone, with the possible exception of the actual Queen.

Probably the most influential and famous of all the French Royal Mistresses was born as Jeanne-Antoinette Poisson in Paris.

It is proven that a clairvoyant predicted that the 9 year old Jeanne-Antoinette would one day become the mistress of King Louis XV and as Jeanne-Antoinette grew up she made a point of seeking out the King, usually by attending royal hunting parties at the nearby forests of Senart.

She did marry in 1741, but did not allow her marriage to get in the way of being around the king as much as she could.

Her endeavors were temporarily spoiled by Marie-Anne de Mailly-Nesle, Marquise de La Tournelle, who was the king's current *"maîtresse en titre"*. The Marquise de La Tournelle quickly grew tired of seeing a beautiful and determined young woman around the Louis XV, and Jeanne-Antoinette had to wait in the shadows until the Marquise de La Tournelle died in 1744 before she could attempt to take the place she believed destiny intended her to have.

Very soon the king became sufficiently enamored with the beautiful and intelligent young woman and made her the official *"maîtresse en titre"* and gave her the official title of "Marquise de Pompadour". Helped along by a most generous financial gift, her husband quickly agreed to an amicable divorce and the Marquise de Pompadour was finally free to live the life she had sought with such intelligence and determination.

Even though her sexual relationship with Louis XV only lasted 6 years, she kept her title of *"maîtresse en titre"* until her death.

This was mainly due to her finely tuned diplomatic skills. She forged important alliances at court and avoided the common mistake made by too many *"maîtresses en titre"* of making an enemy out of The Queen.

Her influence extended far beyond the actual court, however. Not only did she involve herself with cultural aspects of the time, becoming a major supporter of the theatre and especially Moliere, she also advised Louis XV on many points of international politics.

It was the Marquise de Pompadour who advised Louis XV to forge an alliance with Austria against England and Prussia, and it was the Marquise de Pompadour who advised the second ratification of the second contract of Versailles.

Her influence over the king grew, even after she lost her position in his bed to Anne Coupier de Romans, who, adding insult to injury, gave birth to a son fathered by the king.

She spent much of her time and energy on furthering the cases of various writers, amongst them her favorite, Voltaire and Denis Diderot, the author of the French Encyclopedia.

After her death in 1764 she was blamed for many of the mistakes made in the course of the Seven Year War.

Overall she is an example of a mistress who attained and kept the position she wanted by handling herself intelligently and using her powers wisely. If she ever tired of the role she had fought to get so hard there is no evidence of it.

The fact that she kept her title of "*maîtresses en titre*" even when, in reality, her physical relationship with Louis XV had ended speaks volumes of her skills.

Anne Boleyn

Alongside Madame Pompadour, Anne Boleyn is arguably the most influential mistress in history.

Whilst it could be said that Cleopatra would have changed the world of her time even if she had not been involved with Julius Cesar and Mark Antony, Anne Boleyn changed history *because* she was the mistress of Henry VIII.

By the standards of his time, Henry VIII was actually a fairly faithful husband to his wife Catherine of Aragon. Though he had dalliances to be sure, their marriage was for a number of years companionable and loving. Her inability to provide him with a male heir, however, caused him much consternation; without a male heir, the Tudor dynasty would go down in history as hard-won and short-lived, and Henry had a keen awareness of this fact. If Catherine had been able to produce that male heir, history most assuredly would have have taken a radically different path.

In 1525, just as the King's patience with Catherine reached an all-time low, he became seriously enamored with the charismatic young Anne Boleyn, who was, at the time, a member of the Queen's entourage.

Anne Boleyn was actually a very smart young woman, both intellectually and emotionally.

She had caught the king's eye but was well aware that the role of a mere mistress was not what she was after. Having seen her sister Mary Boleyn succumb to the king's advances only to eventually be tossed aside in favor of a new mistress, she decided that only the whole deal was going to do for her.

She resisted the king's advances, which made him even more determined to conquer her. His infatuation grew, and with it her influence over him. Anne made it quite clear that she would only yield to his advances if she were to become his acknowledged queen.

At this point Henry turned his entire passion into getting his marriage to Catherine annulled so he would be free to marry Anne. He tried to get the marriage annulled on the grounds that Catherine's brief previous marriage to his brother Arthur had been consummated, but the Pope refused to grant the annulment until a decision was taken in Rome.

It soon became clear that Henry was not going to get his way via papal channels, so he continued his affair with Anne and exiled Catherine in 1532, moving Anne into The Queen's former quarters.

Anne Boleyn was instrumental in the fall of Cardinal Thomas Wolsey, whose dismissal from office was a direct result of her intrigues. With Wolsey gone Anne quickly gained considerable power over appointments at court and political matters alike.

In 1532 one of her confidantes, a lawyer named Thomas Cromwell, brought before the Court a number of motions which would, in due course, seal the break of England with the Catholic Church and install Henry

VIII as the head of the Church of England.

Henry married Anne in a secret ceremony that same year.

It took another year before The King's marriage to Catherine of Aragon was declared null and void and his marriage to Anne Boleyn officially confirmed.

However, their marriage was not a happy one. Anne also failed to provide the much longed for male child, ironically miscarrying a son when the king was near fatally injured in a jousting accident.

The king had also started to tire of her irritability and her often violent temper. Anne also refused to fit into the more submissive role expected of a Queen at the time. Only a year after the wedding Henry is said to have discussed how he could leave Anne without having to return to Catherine.

When Catherine of Aragon died in 1936 Anne soon realized that her life was in danger. The king was no longer happy with married life, she had not produced an heir and only with both queens dead could he marry someone else. As Anne recovered from her last miscarriage Henry declared that his marriage to her had been an act of witchcraft and Jane Seymour, the king's new mistress, was moved into place.

After Anne was arrested on charges of adultery, incest and high treason; and found guilty, one of the most famous affairs in history came to an end when Anne Boleyn was beheaded in May 1536 on Tower Green.

- 32 -
Support for "Other Women"

When we are in a conventional relationship we usually have access to an enormous amount of support and help when things don't go according to plan. Friends and family are normally more than happy to offer advice or just a shoulder to cry on when things go wrong.

Every bookstore has shelves stacked to the ceiling to help with just about every real or imagined issue that could possibly befall a conventional relationship.

If you look for a book that tells you how to deal with the problems that are specific to having an affair you are in for a long hard search, and what is available tends to just want to lecture you on why it wasn't a bright idea in the first place (a bit late now and you know that anyway). There are a few books in print which deal with the issue, but frankly the ones I have looked at were not written to help us deal with the day-to-day aspects of having an affair.

As the Other Woman we stand pretty much alone.

Our friends and family, if they even know about the affair, are likely to be somewhat less than wholly supportive, and even if they wanted to offer advice they don't usually know what to suggest for the best.

Some Other Women are lucky enough to have a really good friend who has probably been through the same thing, and can at least offer an unconditional shoulder to cry on and advice from her own experience.

But by and large the Other Woman is pretty much expected to cope with the inevitable downsides herself.

While I was researching this book I did a lot of searches on the internet, and found a couple of discussion forums which are a godsend for literally thousands of women who were looking for a non-judgmental place to share their stories and get advice. Often it helps to just find out that we are not alone, that there are probably millions of us all over the world. An anonymous forum is a great platform where Other Women are free to discuss their affairs with others who are in the same or a similar position.

Not all of these forums are really supportive, and some appear to allow rather too much negativity to be expressed about the wives. It pays to look around and "lurk" for a while before jumping into the discussions.

The better ones have a strict "No Wife Bashing" policy and are carefully and strictly moderated to avoid whole discussions sliding down the nasty path of just bitching about people.

After much thought I have decided not to publish the addresses of the better forums here in this book, forums come and go, and a book can't easily be changed once it is in print.

However, I promise to keep a list of the best support-places I have found on the Internet on my website, so if you are looking for something you should be able to find an updated list of the best sites there.

Be aware that all of these forums are run by volunteers who give up their spare time to provide a platform for others to get help and support, so please treat them with respect, and don't just take advice, try and give a little something back by supporting others just as you expect to get support from them.

Be very careful what kind of information you share with others on the Internet however. Not everyone is who they claim to be, and there are some angry wives out there who spend a lot of time and energy researching "Other Women" to the extent of stalking them across the net and eventually publishing details of the women and her married men. This is why the best forums have strict policies regarding the details that can be shared in the general discussions.

Despite those restrictions I have to say I am "wasting" rather a lot of time on my favorite forum and have "met" some amazing women, and made a few real friends there.

If you have any suggestions for helpful websites, other good books or alternative ways we Other Women can get support please just e-mail me via the contact link on the website and I will happily include the information for everyone's benefit!

Postscript

When I first started to write this book I was still reeling from learning about the death of the exceptional man who inspired it. I had no intention of ever getting myself involved with another married man. Quite frankly had anyone suggested that I would do so I may have declared them to be borderline insane.

I was also a touch cynical, having seen a few affairs around me go sour, and having looked a bit more closely at my own family history for clues why affairs are really not such a bright idea.

However, in the course of my research I realized that there are so many women who are living happy and fulfilled lives despite (or maybe even because) being involved with a married man, and so many who could be so much happier with their situation if only they approached the whole subject somewhat differently.

So even at that stage parts of the book were being re-written, added to, and changed. It was started from my own perspective, and then changed as I spoke to more and more men and women.

Every new situation I looked at, every affair I was told about by the people who were or had been conducting it, added to the overall picture. And every one of their stories made me more determined that this book really needed to be finished.

And then, just when I was absolutely not looking to get involved with anyone, let alone with another married man, I met "M."

"M" was and still is just about everything that attracts me to a man. Tall and very handsome, with a wicked sense of humor, intelligent and sensitive, a great person to talk to. Someone to laugh with, smile at and discuss everything under the sun from childhood to music with. My kind of man all round in other words.

I remember very clearly how I felt when I first looked into his eyes. There were immediate butterflies, and the familiar yet almost forgotten feeling we experience when we meet someone who will have a profound influence on our life.

"M," unfortunately however, was and is a married man. For a short while I kidded myself into thinking that we could be "just friends," then, when it became clear that this wasn't going to work, I kidded myself that maybe a "One Night Stand" would "get it out of our system...." Of course it did no such thing so more self-delusion followed and we tried to have just a little fling.

Now, many months later, we are in the middle of a fully blown affair and I am not intending to let that end any time soon if I can possibly help it.

So, finishing this book has become something I was now doing as much for myself as for the women (and men?) who buy it.

Once again I am in that situation where there are no

well defined rules of conduct, and where proper and reasonable advise past the "Don't do it – it will end in tears" platitudes is hard to come by.

I am having to follow my own advise and try to adhere to the rules I have collected over the course of researching this book, gleaned from my own affair and those of others who were kind enough to share their stories.

Whichever course my own current affair will take in the long run, I am determined not to ruin it by making too many of the mistakes that I and others have made in similar situations.

If I can't have the "whole man" I will, at least, make the very best out of the situation I can have, a situation which I have chosen to be in of my own free will and a situation I have entered with my eyes wide open.

In case there are any further editions of this book I may have to revise and update this postscript, but at this stage of both this book and my own life I am just going to say that it is entirely possible to have an affair with a married man and to be happy and fulfilled at the same time.

I am not saying this to show off, or to gloat, or to make myself out to be "The perfect mistress" in any way, shape or form. I am saying it because I am probably not that different to every other "Other Woman" out there. And if I can be in a wonderful affair with a wonderful man and be happy (at least for the time being) with the way things are going then I would hazard a guess that you can, too.

I am managing to have a happy affair by having chosen the man wisely. You can no more have a happy affair with a bad man than have any happy relationship with a bad man! I make sure I don't neglect my friends or my hobbies and I concentrate on my work.

By not sitting around waiting for him to call or be able to see me I am a happier and more contented (and almost certainly a more fun to be with) person when he does.

No, it's not always easy, but then few things that are worth having and doing in life *are* always running smoothly. Occasionally I do get a bit weary and wonder what on earth I am doing (yet again.) But those moments pass.

For the time being I am determined to read my own book whenever we hit a rocky patch, which, admittedly, hasn't really happened yet apart from some slight bumps on the road around Christmas, which is and always will be one of the hardest times for any woman involved with a married man.

So I close the final chapter of this book with a heartfelt "Thank You" to everyone who has helped to make it happen, knowingly or by accident, and especially to the wonderful man who made me brave enough and crazy enough to go where I had really promised myself I would never go again.

I raise my glass to all the Other Women in the world who are bravely loving a married man, and I raise my glass, again, to the wonderful man in my own life, who is making it so much better than it was before I met him!

About the author

Petra Falk (a pseudonym) was born in the late 60's in a small town in Germany. She went to an international boarding school in the Black Forest before going traveling and eventually moving abroad. After many years living in England she returned to her native Germany, where she now lives with her Jack Russell Terrier.

She works in Sales for a multi-national company and her hobbies include writing, traveling, photography and horses.

Petra Falk is divorced from her first (and only) husband and has just started working on her second book.

8555178R0

Made in the USA
Lexington, KY
13 February 2011